Genes for Africa

Genetically modified crops
in the developing world

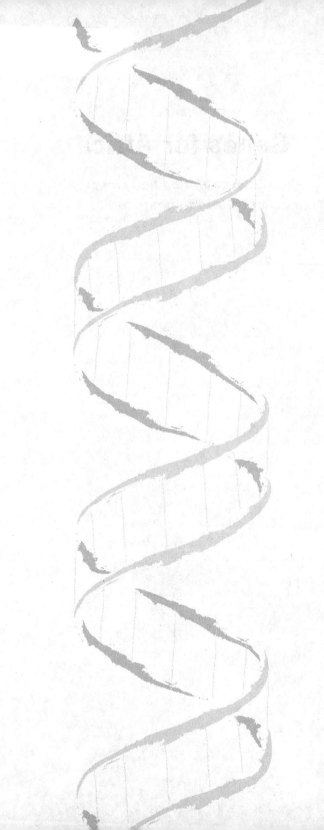

Genes for Africa

Genetically modified crops in the developing world

Jennifer A Thomson

UCT
PRESS

Genes for Africa: Genetically modified crops in the developing world

First published 2002

© UCT Press, 2002
PO Box 24309, Landsdowne 7779

This book is copyright under the Berne Convention. In terms of the Copyright Act, No. 98 of 1978, no part of this book may be reproduced or transmitted in any form or by any means (including photocopying, recording, or by any information storage and retrieval system) without permission in writing from the publisher.

ISBN 1 919 713573

Copy editing by Ally Ashwell
Proofreading by Helena Reid
Design and typesetting by Catherine Crookes
Cover design by Catherine Crookes

Printed and bound in South Africa by Mills Litho, Maitland, Cape Town

Cover photographs © Keith Young/Cape Photo Library,
© Eric Miller/iAfrika

The author and publisher have made every effort to obtain permission for and acknowledge the use of copyright material. Should any infringement of copyright have occurred, please contact the publisher and every effort will be made to rectify omissions or errors in the event of a reprint or new edition.

Contents

Foreword

By Michael Shelby

The issues embedded in the controversy surrounding genetically modified crops (GMCs) are varied and complex. Each is important – human safety, economics, nutrition, international trade policies, intellectual property rights, to name but a few. As with most controversies that play out in the popular press, only the most extreme positions or opinions are clearly visible to the public. In the case of GMCs, we have reassurances from those with a financial stake in the technology that all is well, and allegations from the anti-GMC lobby that these organisms present a clear danger to the environment and human health. The truth, of course, is somewhere in between these two positions, and the public deserves a more factual and reliable source of information on this issue.

Prof. Thomson has written a book based on a thorough and detailed coverage of literature on a wide range of issues related to this controversy. Although it is not a cold and dispassionate treatise on GMCs (of which she is clearly a proponent), it provides a wealth of background information on each of the issues covered, presents the literature sources upon which she bases her conclusions, and employs logical development of her arguments. It will be worthwhile reading for all persons involved in or concerned with the GMC issue. And, it comprises an invaluable source of reference material.

The content and tone of this book are clear reflections of Jennifer Thomson's expertise in this frontier of scientific research and, equally importantly, her deep and abiding concern for the welfare and future of the people of Africa.

The publication of this book will, I believe, be a milestone in efforts to bring the promise of the 'new agriculture' to bear on our world family's solution to hunger and poverty.

Michael D. Shelby, Ph.D.
Chapel Hill, North Carolina, USA
Editor, *Mutation Research*
Staff Scientist, National Institute of Environmental Health Sciences, USA
Past President, Environmental Mutagen Society
January 2001

Foreword

by George Ellis

Scientific study and the associated development of technology have con-
tinually opened up new understandings and associated possibilities to us:
the wheel, fire, pottery, water-borne sewerage, metal smelting, automobiles,
electric power, machine tools, aircraft, vaccines, antibiotics, insulin, plastics,
television, radar, digital computers, laser surgery, to name a few. But
change does not happen without fear and resistance and a lot of focus on
the possible dangers associated with a new technology. Sometimes those
fears have been justified, sometimes not. In the end, it is seldom a black
and white issue. The question is not whether we should adopt the new
technology, but rather how best to use the new opportunities that the new
developments have made available to us. The challenge has been to assess
rationally both the dangers and the opportunities, and then to work out the
best policy for use and control of each new technology.

We have been modifying crops genetically for thousands of years,
indeed ever since agriculture began. A particular new opportunity now
available to us is the development of crops genetically modified using techniques developed by molecular biologists. We call these GM (genetically
modified) crops. The feature of genetic modification is not new; rather it is
the particular molecular biology-based technology that is the innovation.
Here is a case where we have major new opportunities, as a result of our
extraordinary recent understanding of the molecular nature of the mech-
anism of heredity in plants and animals (essentially, the structure of the
DNA and RNA molecules found in the cells of all living things). This allows
highly specific design of new features of existing plants, such as insect and
drought resistance, with an associated increase in agricultural productivity
and hence contribution to reduction of poverty.

But there are also potential dangers and these have certainly generated
a great deal of resistance. Some resistance has been simply irrational – just
a desperate emotional response, evidencing fear of the new without a
considered assessment of the pros and cons. Some of the negative response
has been more considered, focusing specifically on the possible risks of GM
crops, but without considering equally the benefits. Most importantly, these

assessments have not considered the all too clear problems associated with our present day practices. For example, the widespread use of fertilisers, insecticides and broad-band herbicides causes serious pollution of our rivers and dams, damaging aquatic life and threatening our health. One major advantage of GM techniques is that they have the potential to help us avoid this kind of widespread damage to our ecosystems.

The purpose of this book is to present a rational argument about how we can use this new technology safely and to benefit our world. There are two different kinds of dangers to consider. The first danger is based in the nature of the technology and its possible harmful effects on individuals and the environment. Looking at this demands an adequate understanding of molecular biology and of environmental and ecological issues, and requires careful consideration based on a sound scientific understanding of the issues involved. The potential outcome is a set of standards that proposed GM crops should fulfil before being made generally available. GM crops should be tested to determine whether or not they can be used safely in particular circumstances and, if so, the kinds of environments where they may be safely introduced.

The second kind of risk is related to the economics and ethics of the exploitation of GM technology. Specifically, it is possible that its introduction will in practice be yet another way of widening the gap between the rich and the poor. This problem is not based in the particular nature of the technology. Instead there are developmental issues related to any attempt to introduce methods based on high technology into impoverished economies. Solving this issue requires a sound developmental and economic policy, which recognises issues of intellectual rights and the high costs of development and testing, but also insists on providing enhanced opportunity and good pricing to disadvantaged farmers.

Jennifer Thomson is ideally placed to discuss these issues and present the real opportunities and risks. She has widespread experience of the issue in southern Africa, where she has run laboratories at the forefront of research. She has been an invited speaker at conferences on the topic throughout the world. Jennifer Thomson is passionate about her subject and the good it can do for this country and continent. She is also fully aware of the need for safeguards and carefully discusses what those are. She is an excellent guide to the field, who can help us see how to derive real benefits while safeguarding ourselves from the risks.

True environmentalism recognises the need for development, for growing food and making livelihoods available to the poor, and aims to minimise the risks and damage that are entailed. If you want to indulge in thoughtless sloganeering about 'Frankenfoods', then avoid this book, because it will make you think and confront the real issues. You will find the real facts discussed here and placed before you in an enthusiastic but always scientifically carefully controlled way. I can strongly recommend this book as a well thought out and carefully considered presentation of the facts and issues involved.

George Ellis
Department of Mathematics and Applied Mathematics
University of Cape Town
18 July 2000

Reference

Baxter, W. F. (1974) *People or penguins: the case for optimal pollution.* Columbia University Press, New York.

To Mike ...

- -

Acknowledgements

Every aspirant author deserves to have friends like Sandra and Andries Botha, to lend her an enchanting holiday home in idyllic Plettenberg Bay in which to write her book. It was so idyllic that I had to set up my computer looking straight onto a rocky wall or I would never have written a book at all, let alone the first draft of this one in four weeks. Every aspirant author also needs friends who will read the manuscript and make critical comments. My mainstay was Mike Shelby who, noblest of editors, read the first and second drafts. His comments, such as 'would Kaolin or Bosky understand this?' I hope have made *Genes for Africa* accessible to most readers. Grateful thanks also go to Gerald Shaw, former editor of the *Cape Times*, who, late into a jolly dinner party (at Bosky's), rashly offered to read the first draft. Having never studied any form of science, he was the ideal person to force me to simplify. My friend Rion Munting, with whom I studied Zoology at the University of Cape Town and who later became a biology teacher, a potter and a teacher of the science of pottery, was my third editor. Unbelievably she read the book in a single session while recuperating from an operation. My IT 'guru' was Nikki Campbell who assisted ably and cheerfully and sorted out all my computer problems. She also drew all the diagrams and captured all the photographs.

I also want to thank Ally Ashwell, my 'official' editor, who gave it all she had. Sandie Vahl and Glenda Younge from Juta/UCT Press were always enthusiastic and seemed to believe the book would take on a life of its own. And to Marian, my friend from the HERS Summer Institute at Bryn Mawr College, thank you for reading the page proofs in a miraculously short space of time.

- -

Introduction

Genetically modified food: a reasonable approach

During the past couple of years newspaper headlines in many countries have screamed 'Are you eating Frankenstein foods?', 'Beware of genetic pollution!', 'Genetically modified (GM) foods reap a harvest of fears' and 'The dangers of Frankenfoods'. We don't, however, often read headlines such as 'GM rice saves millions of Asian children from blindness', 'GM sweet potatoes save East African crop from virus plague', 'GM cotton gives financial security to South African rural farmers' or 'GM crops prevent starvation in Third World'.

Why is there this bias? Certainly bad news sells newspapers better than good news, but that is not the whole story. One of the reasons could be that the media and public are not aware of the facts behind the fiction. If that is so, scientists are largely to blame. Scientists are traditionally poor communicators, more at ease in their laboratories engaging in discourses with students and colleagues than participating in robust public debate. They would rather write erudite scientific papers to be published in peer reviewed international journals than write a letter to the local newspaper. In contrast, there are many organisations that make a living from supplying the press with scary stories about genetic engineering. Therefore who can blame the public for believing what they read in the popular press?

A scientific perspective

This book aims to present the arguments for genetic engineering. I am a scientist working in South Africa on GM maize, the staple food of many people in sub-Saharan Africa. Two of my research interests are the development of resistance to maize streak virus, a scourge endemic to Africa, and tolerance of plants to drought.

1

It is said that, if past wars were waged over land and political power, the next major conflict will be over water. This is most certainly true of Africa. I have also been involved for many years in regulatory issues around the development and use of GM crops.[1] I like to think, therefore, that I bring experience and a scientific approach to the debate.

Detractors will no doubt say that I have a vested interest in the acceptance and use of GM crops, and this is obviously correct. However, I hope that my training as a scientist allows me to be objective. I therefore highlight the fears about, and objections to, the use of GM crops and foods. In Chapter 5 I try to address such fears and objections from a scientific perspective.

I put my cards clearly on the table: I do not believe that the use of GM crops and foods is the only answer to the problems facing world nutrition — it is just one of many. But I am convinced that genetic modification is a very important part of the answer and should not be thrown out just because we cannot answer every question about long-term safety to human health or the environment. We need to weigh the costs versus the benefits of using GM crops and foods against the costs and benefits of not using these crops and foods.

GM crops and the developing world

The Europeans may be against the introduction of GM crops and foods into Europe. However, the title of this book, *Genes for Africa*, reflects my concern that this should not be used as an argument to prevent their introduction into, and use in, developing countries. As I will discuss, Europe has more than enough food and has a different agenda regarding farmers, providing subsidies for reduced production due to food surplus. Let them not dictate to Africa or any part of the developing world how we should practise agriculture.

At the United Nations Millennium Assembly of Heads of State in September 2000, Secretary General Kofi Annan challenged 'the foremost experts in the world to think through the barrier of low agricultural productivity in Africa. I implore the great philanthropic foundations — which have stimulated so much good and practical research on agriculture

– to rise to this vital challenge' (Annan, 2000, p. 31). Hunger is common-place in sub-Saharan Africa. Of the 600 million people who live there, nearly 200 million are chronically undernourished and some 40 million children are severely underweight. Over 50 million people, mostly children, suffer from vitamin A deficiency and 65% of women of childbearing age are anaemic (Vitamin Information Centre, 1999). Africa is getting poorer and hungrier. Decades of war, weak governments, one-party states and widespread corruption are part of the problem.

These human-made tragedies obscure another, in some ways more enduring, set of problems for African farmers and their families that scientists could help to address (Conway and Sechler, 2000). These include the fact that the technologies developed to boost agricultural production and economic growth during the Green Revolution passed Africa by. Few of the technologies focused on Africa's staple crops or growing conditions. The science that Conway and Sechler refer to includes the development and use of GM crops geared specifically to African needs. I hope that this book will show how such crops can be harnessed to help save the continent from hunger.

Other developing countries also see the advantages of using GM crops. Argentina was second only to the USA in the planting of crops during 1999 and 2000. During 2000 Argentina planted ten million hectares of GM crops compared with 30 million hectares in the USA and only three million hectares in Canada. In China about 1.5 million small-scale farmers have planted insect-resistant cotton, and during 2000 a total of approximately 0.5 million hectares of insect-resistant cotton were planted (James, 2000a and b).

Note

[1] In 1985 I became a member of SAGENE (the South African Genetic Engineering Committee), the body that regulated GMOs until the implementation of the GMO Act in 2001. I chaired the committee from 1990 to 1992 and remained a member until it was dissolved in 1999. I have worked on the development of GM bacteria since 1978 and on GM plants since 1990.

References and further reading

Annan, K. A. (2000) *'We the Peoples': the role of the United Nations in the Twenty-first Century*. United Nations, New York, p. 31.

Conway, G. and Sechler, S. (2000) Helping Africa feed itself. *Science*. Vol. 289, p. 1685.

James, C. (2000a) Global status of commercialized transgenic crops: 1999. *ISAAA Brief*. No. 17. ISAAA, Ithaca, N.Y.

James, C. (2000b) Global review of commercialized transgenic crops: 2000. *ISAAA Brief*. No. 21. ISAAA, Ithaca, N.Y.

Vitamin Information Centre. (1999) Vitamin A: Durban IVACG meeting a key milestone in addressing hidden hunger. *Medical Update*. No. 33.

Chapter 1

Plant breeding and jumping genes

An ancient endeavour

Of all human endeavours, none has had a more profound effect on our history, and on the living world as a whole, than agriculture (Paäbo, 1999). The agricultural revolution, which we believe began in several regions of the world about 10 000 years ago, enabled people to produce and store food. As a result, large communities developed, leading to centralisation of political power and the emergence of complex societies. This in turn paved the way for large-scale warfare, imperialism, industrialisation and almost every other major socio-political development in history. The agricultural revolution had both positive and negative consequences.

These momentous developments relied on the genetic modification of only a handful of plants by early farmers. One of these, maize, is now the second-largest crop in the world. It was domesticated in middle America around 7 500 years ago from a plant called teosinte. This grass looks so different from maize that, until genetic studies showed their close relationship, the two were classified in different genera. Indeed, early maize looked very different from the crop we know today (see Figure 1 in the colour section on page 117).

You would expect that the domestication of maize would have reduced its genetic variation, because early farmers would have selected only a few strains of teosinte with desirable properties. In fact, this is not the case and today maize is genetically more diverse than many other wild or cultivated plants. This indicates that many teosinte genes made it into the maize gene pool through cross-pollination. This may have occurred either during the original process of domestication or afterwards during successive stages of plant breeding. Of course, wild teosinte is still genetically more variable than domesticated maize. The development of teosinte into maize, as we know it today, involved successive rounds of selection of 'good' plants with favourable characteristics. Farmers and plant breeders selected and planted the seeds of these improved varieties, repeating the process over many generations.

Cross-pollination: the transfer of pollen from the flower of one plant to the flower of another related plant. Successful pollination results in fertilisation and seed production.

Cultivar: a cultivated plant variety produced by selective breeding.

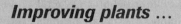

Improving plants …

When people start growing wild plants in cultivation, we call this process 'domestication'. Wild plants seldom produce the high yields of fruit or grains that we require. Consequently, for thousands of years, people have been selecting strains with favourable characteristics and crossing these to produce high-yielding **cultivars**. This is the process of 'plant breeding'.

Recently, molecular biologists have developed new techniques that enable them to introduce genes into crop plants from completely different species and organisms, including bacteria, plants and animals. This process is called 'genetic modification'. It enables scientists to introduce genes from species that are so unrelated to the target plant that it would be impossible to introduce them using conventional plant breeding methods.

The process of plant breeding

Plant breeding is a somewhat different process than natural selection as it involves controlled crosses between selected parent plants. Breeders then evaluate the offspring for the desired improvements.

How does plant breeding work? Breeders take two different varieties of a plant, each of which has individual characteristics or traits that make it attractive; for example, one variety might produce high yields and the other might be resistant to an insect pest. They cross-pollinate these two varieties, collect the seeds and plant them.

6

The plants that grow from these seeds represent a random mix of tens of thousands of genes from each of the parent plants. The breeders then select those plants that show both high yields and insect resistance. Unfortunately, due to the randomness of the process, the selected plants may have acquired an undesirable trait not observed in either parent; for example, the new variety might be sensitive to a **plant virus** that did not affect either parent strain but became a problem when their genes were mixed. These plants would have to be discarded and others found.

> **Plant virus:** an extremely tiny parasite of plants that consists of a core of genes surrounded by a coat of protein.

The story of soybeans

Conventional plant breeding is an extremely inexact and time-consuming process. Thousands or tens of thousands of plants may need to be screened to obtain a plant with the desired characteristics and no undesirable changes. However, an abundance of new crops and crop varieties have been developed in the past 10 000 years using these techniques.

Perhaps the scale of improvement of crops by conventional breeding can best be illustrated by the development of soybeans (Gianessi and Carpenter, 2000). This crop is native to eastern Asia, where it is known to have been cultivated for over 4 000 years. No more than eight soybean cultivars were grown in the United States of America (USA) before 1898. Between 1898 and 1923, more than 1 000 cultivars were introduced, mostly by research stations or grain merchants.

As soybeans became more popular, the United States Department of Agriculture (USDA) sent plant explorers to Asia and by 1947 they had introduced over 10 000 different varieties. Only a limited number of these have been used to develop new cultivars. Soya breeding programmes selected for characteristics such as yield, reduced plant height (for easier harvesting), seed size and quality, oil quality and resistance to insects, **nematodes** and diseases. Genetic improvement resulted in a 25% increase in yield between cultivars released before 1940 and those released after 1970.

Nematode: a round worm; a common plant parasite, found in huge numbers in soil.

These genetic improvements depend on cross-pollination between plants with different characteristics. However, soybean flowers carry both the male and female organs. When the pollen is shed, it drops onto the female part of the same flower, resulting in self-pollination. Fortunately for plant breeders, the stigma (part of the female organ) is receptive to pollen at least one day before the anthers (the male organs) are sufficiently developed to shed pollen. This lag time permits the breeder to introduce pollen from another soybean plant in order to obtain hybrid seed.

Breeding soybeans is a tedious process. The flowers are only about 6 mm long and the plant breeder must use tweezers to transfer pollen from the anthers of the donor plant to the stigma of the recipient flower. One person can cross-pollinate about 50 to 150 flowers per day. Less than half of these are likely to set seed because many flowers abort after the crosses are made.

The role of back-crossing

In any plant breeding process, after the first hybrid offspring has been produced, it is crossed with the parent plant that is being improved. This technique is called **back-crossing**. The parent used in the back-cross is called the *recurrent* parent because it recurs, or is used repeatedly for crossing. The other parent is the *donor* parent because it contributes the desirable gene(s).

During hybridisation, the genes of the donor parent mix with those of the recurrent parent in a random fashion. The purpose of back-crossing is to recover any desirable genes from the recurrent parent that may have been lost in the formation of the original hybrid plant. Each back-cross recovers an additional 50% of the genes of the recurrent parent, amounting to 75% after the first back-cross and 87% after the second. Breeders continue back-crossing until they have recovered the desirable level of genes from the recurrent parent. It usually takes three back-crosses to recover virtually all of the original genes.

Back-crossing: crossing hybrid offspring with the parent plant that is being improved.

Food for thought?

I shall discuss questions around food safety of products derived through conventional breeding in Chapter 6 but they are already worth mentioning here. In an attempt to breed a 'super-broccoli' with high concentrations of a compound known to lower the risk of cancer, plant breeders in the United Kingdom recently crossed normal broccoli with wild Sicilian broccoli (24 May 2000; http://www.agbioworld.org). In this process many hundreds of genes from the wild were introduced into the new variety. We do not know what these genes are or whether they code for any allergenic or toxic compounds. Many plant traits required for survival in the wild may not necessarily be good for human health or agriculture. What are the long-term health and environmental impacts of this broccoli? No one has ever addressed this question and no regulatory body has ever tested the effects of broccoli on food safety or on the environment. If the same broccoli had been developed using **biotechnology**, a whole battery of tests would have been required.

In fact, it has often been claimed that, had many of our current food products been developed through biotechnology, they would never have been accepted as they would not have made it over the regulatory hurdles. This applies to potatoes, which contain a class of toxins called solanine that can be toxic to humans if consumed at high levels. Soybeans and other legumes contain proteins called protease inhibitors, which inhibit enzymes that degrade other proteins. Prior to human consumption, these products must be subjected to processing at high temperatures to inactivate these proteins. Would such food products and food processing requirements have been acceptable had they been introduced by biotechnology? This is indeed food for thought!

biotechnology: the exploitation of biological processes to produce commercially valuable products and processes.

CHAPTER 1: PLANT BREEDING AND JUMPING GENES

Mutations – speeding up the process

What I have described above is the crossing of two plants that, by chance, had developed the characteristic traits that the breeder was looking for. However, breeders can speed up the process by treating plants with agents that can introduce changes (**mutations**) into the DNA. These mutations occur randomly but at a greater rate than normal changes in the DNA, which happen by chance.

The breeder subjects the plant or seeds to agents that cause mutations (**mutagens**) and then selects the plants that express the desired traits, such as increased yield. Mutagens include chemicals and radiation, such as ultra-violet light and X-rays. Thus, the reason why you should avoid excessive exposure to sunlight is that the ultraviolet rays in sunlight can mutate your DNA and this may result in skin cancer.

Good examples of the use of mutagenesis in plant breeding have been the development of plants for improved oil qualities. Plant breeders mutated sunflowers to produce high levels of the nutritionally desirable oleic acid, and flax and canola to have low levels of the nutritionally undesirable linolenic acid (Downey and Robbelen, 1989; Green and Marshall, 1984).

There are many other examples of the successful use of mutagenesis in plant breeding:

- A mutation introduced herbicide resistance into a single soybean cultivar. Traditional crop breeding methods were then used to increase the number of cultivars resistant to herbicides (IAEA, 1995).
- In the Netherlands, irradiation of chrysanthemums introduced a range of new floral colours that quickly replaced previous cultivars (Van Harten, 1998).
- Mutant peanuts containing relatively high levels of monounsaturated oils that promote cardiovascular health are now being grown on a large scale. These peanuts contain 90% of healthy oleic acid and only 5% of linoleic acid, a type of fat associated with cardiovascular disease. Naturally occurring peanuts contain about 50% oleic acid and 40% linoleic acid (23 April 2000; http://www.agbioworld.org).

A 1995 database of the international Food and Agricultural Organisation lists 1 790 varieties of 158 plant species developed through the use of purposely induced mutations. These have been officially released in 52 countries. None of these crops has been subjected to the intense levels of scrutiny that GM crops in commercial use have undergone.

When breeders induce mutations they are likely to discover useful traits that do not exist in natural populations. However, even with the help of mutagens, mutation remains a random process that is limited in terms of the type of traits that can be created. Mutagenesis thus rarely produces the particular desired characteristics.

DNA: deoxyribonucleic acid, the complex molecule that makes up genes and chromosomes and stores genetic information.

Mutation: an inheritable change in DNA; in other words, the change gets passed on from one generation to the next.

Mutagen: an agent that causes mutations.

Conventional breeding can produce toxins

Many wild plants contain toxic compounds that have evolved, for example, as defence mechanisms against predators. Through the ages, a major goal of plant breeding has been to reduce or eliminate these toxins. The wild potato (*Solanum acaule*) is the progenitor of cultivated varieties. It contains a potentially toxic compound at concentrations about three times that of cultivated strains. Similarly, the wild cabbage (*Brassica oleracea*) is the progenitor of cabbage, broccoli, and cauliflower. Its leaves contain about twice the level of potential toxins compared to cultivated cabbage. Similar reductions in toxicity through plant breeding have been reported in lettuce, lima bean, mango and cassava.

In contrast, there are several well-documented examples where plant breeding has inadvertently introduced higher levels of toxins. In order to reduce the use of synthetic chemical pesticides, plant breeders have developed plants that are more resistant to insects. However, these plants often contain high levels of natural toxins, some of which they use to repel insects. A new variety of highly insect-resistant celery was introduced in

America. Centers for Disease Control from all over the country received a flurry of complaints because people who handled the celery developed rashes and burns when their skin was subsequently exposed to sunlight. Some detective work found that the pest-resistant celery contained 6 200 parts per billion (ppb) of **carcinogenic** and mutagenic substances called **psoralens**, instead of the 800 ppb present in normal celery (Ames *et al.*, 1990). In another case, a new potato, developed at a cost of millions of dollars, had to be withdrawn from the market because of its acute toxicity to humans. This was due to two natural toxins, **solanin** and **chaconine**, that block nerve transmission (*ibid.*).

Many such toxic plant varieties never come to market as they are detected by the quality control procedures of the seed companies. As mentioned above, stricter approval procedures for crops produced by genetic modification significantly reduce the likelihood of such mishaps (Butler and Reichhardt, 1999).

Carcinogen: a compound that can cause cancer.

Chaconine: a plant compound that blocks nerve transmission.

Psoralen: a compound found in many plants that can make humans and animals more sensitive to exposure to light.

Solanin: a plant compound that blocks nerve transmission.

Jumping genes

One characteristic that has assisted plant breeders, although they did not know it until fairly recently, is the fact that DNA is inherently 'plastic'; in other words, DNA is not a rigid molecule but it can undergo considerable rearrangements. Barbara McClintock, a maize geneticist, first described such rearrangements in the 1950s (McClintock, 1951). She noticed something odd going on with her maize plants. Sometimes the patterns of pigmented spots in the seeds of the offspring differed from those in either of their parents. These changes could not be explained by classical **Mendelian genetics**. Moreover, these patterns could change back again in subsequent generations.

The cause of these changes are elements of DNA that can 'jump' around the **chromosomes**. McClintock called them 'transposable elements' or '**transposons**' but we can simply call them 'jumping genes'.

Gregor Mendel (1822–1884) developed the principles of heredity based on his research on peas. He used his findings to explain the behaviour of 'factors', now called genes, from generation to generation. In today's terms, Mendel's first law states that cells, except for eggs and sperm, contain two copies of each gene. Eggs and sperm have only one copy and therefore need to fuse during fertilisation to produce an offspring. Mendel's second law states that pairs of genes are located on pairs of chromosomes that occur independently in the cell.

Mendelian genetics: laws of heredity proposed by the Austrian monk, Gregor Mendel, in the nineteenth century

Chromosome: a structure composed of a very long molecule of DNA that carries hereditary information. Humans have 23 pairs of chromosomes.

Transposon (jumping gene): a mobile genetic element, consisting of a gene or series of genes, that can insert itself at random into chromosomes.

Unfortunately, McClintock's theory of transposons was rejected by scientists of the day. Eveylen Fox Keller (1983) explains the reasons for this in a spellbinding biography entitled *A feeling for the organism*. That 'feeling' was McClintock's greatest strength, but unfortunately for the acceptance of her theory, also her greatest weakness. Other scientists just did not share McClintock's feeling for her maize. Because they could not understand the complexity of the system she described, they chose to reject her theory out of hand. It was only when jumping genes were discovered in bacteria, a much simpler system, that scientists realised that she had been correct all along. Barbara McClintock received the Nobel Prize for this discovery in 1983.

Jumping genes certainly increase the variability of DNA in an organism. We call this the plasticity of an organism's **genome**. It provides breeders increased diversity with which to work. It was this unfettered jumping around of genes that caused another Nobel Laureate, Werner Arber, to wonder aloud whether the bacteria we work with today are the same as the ones we worked with yesterday (W. Arber, personal communication, 1978). Fortunately, nature has evolved mechanisms of 'damping down' jumping genes so that they do not create havoc in the genome.

Readers should be aware that the random jumping around of pieces of DNA is a natural process. People opposed to the use of GM crops should note this before they condemn scientists for randomly inserting DNA into plants. The same process is happening constantly all around us in nature.

Genome: the genetic composition of an organism.

In summary ...

Conventional breeding, with or without the use of mutagens, has yielded a vast array of superior crops. However, sometimes this process can result in plants with increased levels of toxins or with other undesirable attributes. Conventional plant breeding is assisted by the inherent plasticity of DNA, due to the fact that genes are able to jump around and insert in different places. Despite this, plant breeding is a slow, tedious process. It is also inexact, as the genes from both parents mix randomly. Genetic engineering can speed up the development of new, improved crops in a more precise manner. I discuss this further in Chapter 2.

References and further reading

Ames, B. N., Profet, M. and Gold, L. S. (1990) Nature's chemicals and synthetic chemicals: comparative toxicology. *Proceedings of the National Academy of Sciences, USA*. Vol. 87, pp. 7782–7786.

Butler, D. and Reichhardt, T. (1999) Long-term effect of GM crops serves up food for thought. *Nature*. Vol. 398, pp. 651–656.

Downey, R. K. and Robbelen, G. (1989) *Brassica* species. In: Robbelen, G., Downey, R. K. and Ashri, A. (eds) *Oil crops of the world*. McGraw-Hill, New York, pp. 339–362.

Gianessi, L. P. and Carpenter, J. E. (2000) *Agricultural biotechnology: benefits of transgenic soybeans*. Report for National Center for Food and Agricultural Policy (ncfap@ncfap.org).

Green, A. G. and Marshall, D. R. (1984) Isolation of induced mutants in linseed (*Linum usitatissimum*) having reduced linolenic acid content. *Euphytica*. Vol. 33, pp. 321–328.

IAEA. (1995) *Induced mutations and molecular techniques for crop improvement: proceedings of a symposium, Vienna, 19–23 June 1995*. International Atomic Energy Agency, Vienna.

Keller, E. F. (1983) *A feeling for the organism*. W. H. Freeman and Company, New York.

McClintock, B. (1951) Chromosome organization and genic expression. *Cold Spring Harbor Symposium on Quantitative Biology*. Vol. 16, p. 40.

Paäbo, S. (1999) Neolithic genetic engineering. *Nature*. Vol. 398, pp. 194–195.

Van Harten, A. M. (1998) *Mutation breeding: theory and practical applications*. Cambridge University Press, Cambridge.

Van Rensburg, J. B. J. (undated) *The history of maize*. Summer Grain Centre, Potchefstroom.

Chapter 2

What is genetic modification of plants?

Genetic engineering – the basics

As discussed in the previous chapter, conventional plant breeding has been practised for centuries and has succeeded in producing a wide variety of commercial plants and crops with a range of important agricultural traits. It has succeeded in converting a Mexican grass into maize and a Middle Eastern grass into wheat. However, it is to a large extent a hit-or-miss process, combining large parts of plant genomes in a rather uncontrolled fashion. Furthermore, the rate of increase in crop yields due to conventional breeding is slowing down. We need additional options to keep pace with growing demands for food. Genetic engineering allows scientists to transfer well-characterised and specific genes into plants, resulting in the introduction of one or more defined traits into a particular genetic background. This process is called 'plant transformation' and the genes involved are expressed to produce **proteins** responsible for the particular trait. An added advantage is that the transferred **gene**(s), or **transgene**(s), can come from any **organism**.

Gene: the biological unit of inheritance that transmits hereditary information and controls the appearance of a physical, behavioural or biochemical trait. It is composed of DNA and consists of a series of bases comprising its genetic code.

Organism: an individual plant, animal or micro-organism (e.g. a bacterium) that can independently carry out life functions.

Protein: a molecule consisting of amino acids. The sequence of the amino acids is encoded in the gene for that particular protein. Proteins can be enzymes (biological catalysts) or structural proteins (keratin that forms the basis of hair and feathers is a structural protein).

Transgene: a gene transferred from one organism to another by genetic engineering.

Input and output traits

Most traits transformed into plants to date involve herbicide tolerance and resistance to viral, bacterial and fungal diseases, as well as resistance to herbivorous insects. These so-called **input traits** are characteristics that improve the productivity of a crop and decrease dependency on chemical pesticides and herbicides. They are therefore mainly of benefit to seed companies and farmers. However, the environment also benefits because of the decrease in the use of pesticides. These traits will be discussed further in Chapter 3. The second generation or **output traits** include improvements to the quality of foods, delayed ripening of fruit and vegetables, and the production of vitamin A in rice. They have a more direct benefit to consumers and will be discussed in greater detail in Chapter 4. This chapter explains how these input and output traits are introduced into plants. It will cover the basic details of how **transgenic plants** (plants carrying introduced genes) are made.

Input trait: a characteristic that improves the productivity of a crop and decreases dependency on inputs like chemical pesticides and herbicides.

Output trait: an improvement in the quality of the food or crop produced that is of benefit to consumers.

Transgenic plant: a plant into which a gene from another species of plant, or another organism (e.g. a bacterium), has been transferred.

At present most transgenic plants contain only one or a few transgenes as the traits involved usually depend on the expression of a single gene. However, in future, genetic engineering of plants is likely to involve traits encoded by a number of different genes. This will require more complicated genetic engineering techniques but the basic principles outlined in this chapter will still hold.

DNA, genes and their functions

Before explaining how new genes are inserted into plants, it is probably a good idea to cover some basic facts about DNA, genes and how they function in an organism. James Watson and Francis Crick discovered the structure of DNA in 1953. The story is told in a fascinating book by James Watson called *The double helix* (Watson, 1968). The structure of the DNA molecule looks like a double helix: two chains wrapped around each other rather like a spiral staircase (see Figure 2 in the colour section on page 117). The two strands of DNA are held together by **base pairing.**

The steps of the DNA staircase consist of four chemical **bases**: adenine, thymine, guanine and cytosine. These bases are arranged in various permutations that constitute the **genetic code**. This is an alphabet which, despite relying on only four letters, delivers messages to the cell that enable it to behave in different ways.

Base: DNA has four chemicals called bases that form the 'rungs' of the ladder of the double helix: adenine, thymine, cytosine and guanine. The genetic code is determined by the sequence of the bases.

Base pairing: the links between the bases on the matching 'rungs' of the double helix. In DNA, adenine pairs with thymine and cytosine with guanine. It is this base pairing that holds the two strands of DNA together, forming the double helix.

Genetic code: the sequences of bases on a DNA molecule.

A gene is a sequence of DNA that has a start, a middle and an end. Genes carry the coded information that enables the cell to make proteins. Proteins include both structural proteins like the keratin in hair and skin, and **enzymes** that control the biochemical processes in the cell. Protein synthesis is the process by which a cell manufactures the proteins it requires.

During protein synthesis, an enzyme first recognises the start of the gene coding for the required protein. The enzyme then makes a copy of one strand of the DNA in that gene. This copy is in the form of a very similar molecule called RNA, which, unlike DNA, is a single strand. This process of rewriting the DNA into a different form is called **transcription**. The RNA molecule is called messenger RNA (mRNA) as it carries a message from the DNA to the rest of the cell.

In the next stage, the cell 'reads' the genetic code in the mRNA and produces a protein made up of a sequence of units called **amino acids**. This process is called **translation** as it translates the code into its final form. The term **gene expression** is used to describe the overall process whereby information present in DNA is converted into a protein. The processes of transcription and translation are shown diagrammatically in Figure 3 on the next page.

Amino acid: the basic unit of a protein. There are 20 different kinds of amino acids. Proteins consist of chains of amino acids in the order laid down by the gene that codes for that protein.

Enzyme: a protein that acts as a catalyst to enable a biochemical reaction to take place. The enzyme itself is not changed in the process.

Gene expression: the process whereby a gene is transcribed into mRNA and then translated into a protein.

RNA: ribonucleic acid. It is a molecule synthesised from DNA in a process called transcription.

Transcription: the synthesis of RNA from DNA.

CHAPTER 2: WHAT IS GENETIC MODIFICATION OF PLANTS?

Translation: the process by which a particular sequence of bases in messenger RNA (mRNA) determines the sequence of amino acids in a protein.

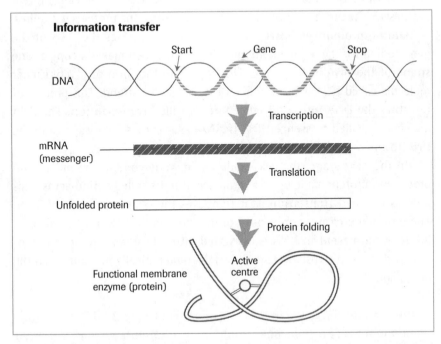

FIGURE 3: Gene expression is the process whereby information in DNA is transcribed into messenger RNA, from which it is translated into a protein. The gene is said to code for the protein.

DNA is generally found in the nuclei of plant and animal cells, where it forms strands known as chromosomes. A gene is a segment of DNA on a chromosome. In the laboratory, enzymes can be used to cut particular genes out of chromosomes. The excised gene can then be spliced into another piece of DNA. In this way genes can be transferred into plants in a process called **plant transformation.**

Plant transformation: the process whereby any gene can be introduced into a plant. Such a plant is then known as a transgenic plant.

Plant transformation

Plant transformation is possible because plant cells are **totipotent**. This means that a single, isolated plant cell can grow into an entirely new plant; for example, if a single cell of a carrot is put into tissue culture, a whole new carrot plant can regenerate, or grow out of it. Thus if a gene is transferred into this isolated plant cell, every cell of the regenerated plant will contain that gene.

This is, however, not true of animals or humans. You cannot take a finger cell and grow a whole person from it! This is because animals are not genetically capable of being totipotent. One way to think about this is to imagine that a cell from an adult plant has a 'genetic memory' of when it was first formed at fertilisation. Such a cell, when placed in tissue culture, 'remembers' what it was like to develop into an adult plant and does so. Figure 4 (see page 118 in the colour section) shows shoots and roots developing from single cells in tissue culture.

In practice, before the required gene is introduced into the plant DNA, it is spliced next to a 'marker gene' that codes for resistance to a **herbicide** or to an **antibiotic**. The plant receiving the genes is naturally sensitive to the particular herbicide or antibiotic. Thus only transformed cells that contain and express the genes for herbicide or antibiotic resistance will be able to grow on the tissue culture medium. The use of **antibiotic resistance genes** in plant genetic engineering has been the subject of considerable controversy and will be discussed in Chapter 5.

Totipotent: the ability of a single cell to form a complete organism. A single plant cell can develop into an adult plant because its cells are totipotent.

Herbicide: a chemical compound that kills weeds.

Antibiotic: a substance isolated from a micro-organism that destroys or inhibits the growth of other micro-organisms, especially disease-causing bacteria and fungi. Many antibiotics are made synthetically.

Transformed plant cells are placed on a gel-like medium containing the selected herbicide or antibiotic. They divide into an undifferentiated mass of cells called **callus**, but only callus expressing the genes for resistance to the herbicide or antibiotic will grow. Plant hormones such as auxin and cytokynin are used to trigger plants to develop from the transformed callus. Once plants are fully developed they are taken out of the medium and planted in soil for 'hardening off'. The process is shown in Figure 5 below.

Antibiotic resistance gene: a gene coding for resistance to an antibiotic. Such genes are often used in the production of transgenic plants as transformed plants will grow in the presence of the antibiotic and non-transformed ones will be killed.

Callus: a mass of relatively unspecialised tissue used in plant tissue culture as the starting material for the propagation of plant clones. A clone is a group of genetically identical cells or organisms.

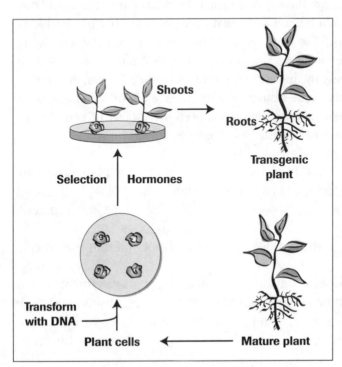

Figure 5: The process of plant transformation. Plant material is transformed with DNA carrying the gene of interest and a selectable marker. Callus tissue develops on selective tissue culture media. Shoots develop following the addition of plant growth hormones. Withdrawal of these hormones promotes root development.

Monocot and dicot plants

Flowering plants can be divided into two groups: **dicotyledonous** plants (dicots) and **monocotyledonous** plants (monocots). Dicots are plants that develop from two (di) cotyledons in the seed. They can be recognised by the branching veins in their leaves. Commercially valuable dicots include many horticultural plants such as petunias, and crops like tobacco, tomatoes, cotton, soybeans and potatoes. Monocots develop from a single (mono) cotyledon in the seed and can be recognised by the parallel veins in their leaves. Most of the world's crops are grains, which are all monocots, including maize, wheat, rye and sorghum. Monocots and dicots are transformed by different processes.

Dicotyledonous plants (dicots): plants that develop from two (di) cotyledons in the seed. They can be recognised by the branching veins in their leaves. Examples are tomatoes and petunias.

Monocotyledonous plants (monocots): plants that develop from a single (mono) cotyledon in the seed. They can be recognised by the parallel veins in their leaves. Examples are maize and wheat.

Transformation of dicotyledonous plants

Agrobacterium tumefaciens is a soil **bacterium** that may be harmful to dicots. It makes a tumour on plants it infects (*tumefaciens* is derived from the Latin for 'swollen'). Because these tumours are often found in the crown region of the root, the disease is called Crown Gall. Scientists were amazed to discover that when these bacteria infect a plant, they transfer part of their DNA into the plant cells where it becomes integrated into the plant's genetic material. Not long after this discovery, scientists realised that the introduction of a foreign gene into *A. tumefaciens* DNA would enable its transfer to the plant cell nucleus. This led to the development of dicot plant transformation.

Bacterium: a small, single-celled organism lacking a nucleus.

CHAPTER 2: WHAT IS GENETIC MODIFICATION OF PLANTS?

The process of dicot plant transformation takes three to four months and involves the following steps:

- Cut small discs from the leaves of the plant and place them in dishes containing a liquid medium.
- Inoculate the surface of the leaf discs with *A. tumefaciens* bacteria containing the gene to be transferred to the plant and incubate for two to three days.
- Transfer the leaf discs to selection medium containing the herbicide or antibiotic of choice.
- Transformation occurs along the cut edges of the discs where a mass of undifferentiated cells called callus tissue forms.
- Transfer the callus tissue to a different medium, also containing the antibiotic or herbicide, which allows only resistant transgenic plants to develop.
- Add growth hormones to promote the growth of a plant from the callus tissue.
- Withdraw the hormones to promote root development.

We know little about how these bacterial genes are integrated into the DNA of plant cells. It appears to be a random process and much research is being done to understand how it works. Scientists are also investigating ways of integrating genes at specific target sites in the plant DNA. Examples of transformed dicot plants include:

- petunias producing a range of attractive flower colors and patterns;
- tomatoes with delayed ripening;
- cotton resistant to insect pests and herbicides;
- soybeans with improved oil quality and tolerance towards herbicides; and
- potatoes resistant to viruses and insects.

Transformation of monocotyledonous plants

Initially, *A. tumefaciens* was unable to transfer DNA into monocots efficiently. Therefore these plants were usually transformed by a process called particle bombardment or **biolistics**, a word derived from the words **biological ballistics**. This is because the early prototypes of the apparatus resembled a gun and the genes were propelled into the plant by gunpowder. The apparatus, although now powered by helium gas, is still called a 'gene gun'.

To transform plants biolistically, DNA carrying the genes to be transformed into the plant is coated onto tiny, chemically inert metal particles, usually gold or tungsten. The gene gun is used to shoot these particles into the plant cells. A number of instruments are available for use in biolistics, based on various accelerating mechanisms. Figure 6A (see page 119 in the colour section) shows the most widely used gene gun, currently marketed by Bio-Rad, Inc (Biolistics®). After 'bombardment' the plant cells are regenerated into plants using a technique similar to dicot transformation, which is described above. Figure 6B shows the effect of introducing genes for herbicide resistance into a maize plant using biolistics.

> **Biolistics:** the process whereby genes are 'shot' into monocot plant cells using a device powered by helium gas. The word biolistics is derived from the words **biological ballistics** as early versions of the apparatus looked like a gun and were powered by gunpowder. The device is still called a 'gene gun'.

The use of promoters

In order for a foreign gene to be expressed (to make its protein product), the plant must recognise it and be able to 'read' the gene as if it were one of its own. In particular, the plant needs to recognise the start of the gene (see Figure 3, page 20). The sequence of DNA that is recognised as being the start of a gene is called a **promoter**. Promoters define if, when, where and how much protein a gene will produce. Dicots and monocots have different promoters. These must be present if the gene is to be 'read' in the respective plant groups.

One of the earliest promoters to be used in the transformation of dicots is still widely used. It is the 35S promoter of the cauliflower mosaic virus, commonly referred to as the 35S promoter (Kay *et al.*, 1987). In monocots the promoter of choice is usually derived from a maize ubiquitin gene and is therefore called the ubiquitin promoter (Christensen and Quail, 1996).

It is often advantageous to develop a transgenic plant in which the gene of interest is expressed only in certain tissues or under certain conditions; for example, genes that cause delayed ripening of fruit should be expressed in the cells of the fruit only. Similarly, only stalk cells need to express the gene for resistance to a stalk borer. To achieve this we use specific promoters that are only recognised in a particular tissue or part of the plant. A tissue-specific promoter has been used to improve the nutritional value of rice, the staple food for more than two billion people in Asia. It makes a lot of sense for the gene to produce the nutritional protein only in the rice kernels that people eat, and not in the leaves or roots of the plant. On the other hand, if we wanted to produce rice plants resistant to a fungal disease, we would want the anti-fungal protein to be expressed in the leaves, stems and other vegetative parts of the rice plant.

A novel way of detecting whether a particular promoter is able to express a gene in the desired tissue is to fuse it to a reporter gene that can be seen by the naked eye. One such gene is the luciferase gene that is responsible for the 'light' produced by the firefly (Ow *et al.*, 1986). You can then actually see which plants have been transformed as they actually glow in the dark! This technique also allows us to see in which particular tissues the gene is expressed.

Promoter: the part of the DNA that 'informs' the cell that 'the gene starts here'. This is the region of the DNA where the enzyme that transcribes the DNA into RNA begins to act.

In summary ...

Genetic modification of plants involves the introduction of genes taken from any organism into plant cells. This can be accomplished using either the bacterium *Agrobacterium tumefaciens* or a 'gene gun'. Growth of these cells on selective media results in the regeneration of whole plants, each of which carries the introduced genes. Depending on which promoters are used, these genes may either be expressed in the whole plant all the time or in individual tissues under specific circumstances.

References and further reading

Christensen, A. H. and Quail, P. H. (1996) Ubiquitin promoter-based vectors for high-level expression of selectable and/or screenable marker genes in monocotyledonous plants. *Transgenic Research.* Vol. 5, pp. 213–218.

Kay, R., Chan, A., Daly, M. and McPherson, J. (1987) Duplication of CaMV 35S promoter sequences creates a strong enhancer for plant genes. *Science.* Vol. 236, pp. 1299–1302.

Ow, D. W., Wood, K. V., DeLuca, M., De Wet, J. R., Helinski, D. R. and Howell, S. H. (1986) Transient and stable expression of the firefly luciferase gene in plant cells and transgenic plants. *Science.* Vol. 234, pp. 856–859.

Watson, J. D. (1968) *The double helix.* Weidenfeld and Nicolson, London.

Chapter 3

First generation GM crops

Benefiting the producers

Much of the controversy around genetically modified (GM) crops currently on the market concerns the so-called 'first generation' GM crops. Most of these crops have been modified for resistance to insect pests, **herbicides** (weedkillers) and viruses. It is not difficult to see why they were the first to be developed. In retrospect, however, it might have been a good idea if, in parallel to these first generation GM crops, the seed companies had developed crops that more clearly benefited the consumer.

> **Herbicide:** a compound (weedkiller) that kills unwanted vegetation such as weeds. Unfortunately these compounds are often also toxic to crops.

One of the reasons why pest- and herbicide-resistant crops were developed first is the fact that genes conferring these traits are relatively easy to isolate. Many of them are derived from soil bacteria that produce proteins that are toxic to insects or that detoxify the herbicides that the bacteria encounter in their environments.

Scientists used these genes to develop the techniques of genetic modification of crops. The companies that developed these initial products were agricultural companies, which focused on developing products specifically to help farmers. The process of establishing these techniques was long and expensive, so it is perfectly understandable that seed companies wished to sell seeds that would directly profit both their established customers, the farmers, as well as help them recoup their development costs. We can therefore think of these first generation GM crops as containing 'input' value genes that benefit the farmers and seed companies. In fact, most of the profits go directly to the grower (Traxler and Falck-Zepeda, 1999). Second generation GM crops (see Chapter 4) contain 'output' value genes that directly benefit the consumer. However, as I will discuss in Chapter 10, in developing countries it is often difficult to draw distinctions between farmers and consumers.

This chapter deals with plant resistance to insects, herbicides and viruses. It also considers the highly emotive case of the so-called 'terminator technology' genes.

Insect-resistant crops

Insect pests, like the cotton bollworm, corn and maize borers, and the potato beetle, devastate many crops worldwide. In South Africa, sugarcane farmers experience huge losses due to the sugarcane borer. Therefore farmers resort to spraying extensively with expensive chemical insecticides. This is often done using aeroplanes with the result that a great deal of spray drifts away from the target crops. These insecticides can adversely affect the health of farm workers and their families. They also have devastating effects on non-target insects. And how effective is crop spraying? All the pests mentioned above, except the potato beetle, effect their damage inside the crop plant. In other words, the insect larvae bore into the plant and decimate it from the inside. Thus spraying insecticide from the outside is rather like shutting the stable door after the horse has bolted. It is not very effective. Furthermore, more than 90% of the chemical insecticide applied does not even come in contact with the plant but ends up on the soil.

Natural insecticides from soil bacteria

What genetic engineering offers is the introduction of a gene that enables the plant to produce a protein toxin that kills a given insect pest. The plant produces this protein *inside* the plant, precisely where the insect larvae are feeding. The gene chosen for this purpose comes from a naturally occurring soil bacterium, *Bacillus thuringiensis* (*Bt*). *Bt* formulations, consisting of either the bacteria themselves or the proteins they produce, have been used for more than four decades as non-chemical insecticides. The bacterium produces a non-toxic protein that is activated by enzymes in the gastrointestinal tract of certain insect larvae to form a toxin. This toxin binds to specific sites in the lining of the insect's gut, where it produces a hole. This perforation results in the rapid death of the insect.

There are many varieties of *Bt* bacteria, all producing slightly different toxins that bind to specific receptors in different insects. However, many can be grouped together as being toxic to, among others, Lepidoptera (butterflies and moths), Diptera (flies) and Coleoptera (beetles). Other animals and humans lack these specific receptors, so *Bt* is not toxic to them. In fact, even insects that are not closely related to the target insects lack these receptors and therefore remain unaffected. Thus, many beneficial insects killed by chemical insecticides are left unaffected by *Bt* crops. Figure 7 shows the process whereby the *Bt* **toxin** is activated in the larval gastrointestinal tract and kills the insect.

Bt **toxin:** a protein toxin produced by the soil bacterium *Bacillus thuringiensis*, which kills insect larvae. *Bt* toxins are not toxic to other animals or humans.

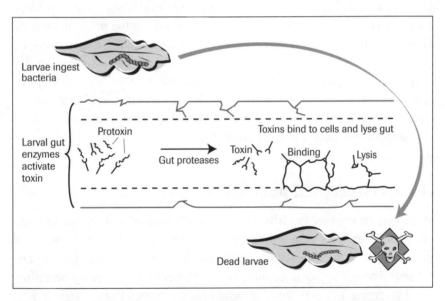

FIGURE 7: This diagram illustrates how an insect larva ingests a *Bt* pro-toxin and activates it by cutting it with specific protease enzymes. The active toxin binds to specific receptors on the larval gastrointestinal tract lining, makes pores in the wall and kills the insect.

Although spray formulations based on the *Bt* bacteria have been in commercial use since the late 1950s, their use is constrained by the fact that the toxic proteins are unstable in the presence of sunlight. In addition, many of the insect larvae burrow into the plants they devour. Thus spraying the *Bt* toxin onto the surface of the plant does not necessarily mean that it reaches its target. The advantage of transgenic plants producing the *Bt* toxin themselves is that they deliver the toxin directly to the feeding insects. Figure 8 (see page 120 in the colour section) shows the effect of *Bt* protection on potatoes.

Bt maize, cotton and potatoes were introduced commercially in 1995/1996 and, according to reports by Clive James (1997; 1998; 1999), were grown on approximately 10 million acres in 1997, 20 million in 1998 and 30 million in 1999. The extremely rapid adoption of the insect-resistant crops demonstrates the outstanding grower satisfaction with their performance. The Economic Research Service of the United States Department of Agriculture reports that the use of certain *Bt* crops is associated with 'significantly higher yields' and 'fewer insecticide treatments for target pests' (Klotz-Ingram *et al.*, 1999).

A report by Gianessi and Carpenter (1999) notes that in 1998 the planting of *Bt* corn seed in the USA saved two million acres from being sprayed with insecticides against the European corn borer. In the same year, the planting of *Bt* cotton resulted in 5.3 million fewer insecticide treatments, saving a total of 0.9 million kilograms of chemical insecticides. Yield increases resulting from reduced crop damage totaled 38.6 million kilograms. The overall net benefit to cotton producers in the USA was an increase of $92 million. In their most recent report, Gianessi and Carpenter (2001) state that, in the USA, farmers who grew *Bt* cotton varieties eliminated 15 million units of insecticide spray compared to growers who grew conventional varieties. This resulted in a reduction in chemical insecticide use of 1.2 million kilograms and generated an incremental $99 million in net income. Farmers who planted *Bt* corn saved one million acres from treatment with chemical insecticides.

Ron Smith (1999), an entomologist from Auburn University in Alabama, credits *Bt* cotton technology with having '... saved the cotton industry in Alabama and in other geographic areas that historically favor high budworm pressure' (p.18). There have also been reports of dramatic decreases in the use of insecticides from Australia (43%) (Monsanto, 1999) and China (60–80%) (Xia *et al.*, 1999). It is projected that these decreases will continue. Kline and Company (2000), a New Jersey-based consulting firm, project that the planting of *Bt* crops will result in a cumulative reduction of 5.9 million kilograms of insecticide active ingredient by 2009.

In South Africa, trials on *Bt* cotton and maize have been undertaken in a number of areas. Scientists compared field and commercial trials of *Bt* cotton with neighbouring fields of non-*Bt* cotton. The results showed that there was an average increase in yield of 485 kilograms per hectare (between 18 and 27%) together with an average of 4.6 fewer insecticide applications (Bennett *et al.*, 2001). The acceptance of *Bt* cotton by small-scale farmers in the Makhatini Flats area of KwaZulu-Natal has been dramatic. In 1997 only four participated. In 1998 this increased to 75, with 200 hectares under cultivation. By the year 2000 the number totaled 644, with 1250 hectares being planted. This accounts for approximately 50% of the total area planted to cotton in that region (J. Webster, Executive Director AfricaBio, personal communication, 2001).

The effect of *Bt* on non-target insects, animals and humans

Bt proteins have little or no effect on natural insect predators and parasites. This is the conclusion of extensive laboratory and field studies in the USA conducted, amongst others, with lady beetles, green lacewings, parasitic wasps and other arthropods (e.g. Dogan *et al.*, 1996). The decrease in the use of insecticides allows beneficial insects and other organisms to survive among *Bt* crops where they can help to control secondary pests, which are often a problem when high levels of insecticides are used. Similar results have been found in China where the reduction in insecticide use resulted in an average increase of 24% in the number of insect predators (Xia *et al.*, 1999). In South Africa there is anecdotal evidence of an increase in both insects and birds following the planting of *Bt* crops. In addition, three species of frogs, which are no longer found in fields of non-*Bt* cotton are now resident in *Bt* cotton fields, thanks to the decreased use of insecticides (J. Webster, personal communication, 2001).

An added bonus resulting from the use of *Bt* crops, especially maize, is the reduction in post-harvest spoilage due to fungal infection. Storage of insect-damaged maize in the warm conditions prevalent in many parts of Africa results in the rapid growth of fungi. Apart from damaging the maize, some of these fungi produce extremely toxic compounds. Mycotoxins (myco = mould) include aflatoxins, which, unlike *Bt*, are highly toxic to people and animals. *Bt*-protected maize contains lower levels of fumonisin, a fungal toxin that can be fatal to livestock (Norred, 1993) and that is associated with human oesophageal cancer in parts of South Africa (Marasas *et al.*, 1988). Scientists (Munkvold *et al.*, 1997; 1999) have shown that the rotting of maize cobs due to fungal infection is dramatically reduced in *Bt* maize. Up to a 96% reduction has been observed (Figure 9A). This is accompanied by an equally dramatic (up to 93%) decrease in levels of the toxic fumonisin (Figure 9B). The authors conclude that 'genetic engineering of maize for insect resistance may enhance its safety for animal and human consumption'. Similar reductions have been reported by Dowd (2000) of the United States Department of Agriculture, and by Cahagnier and Melcion (2000) and Pietri and Piva (2000) in Italy, Spain and France.

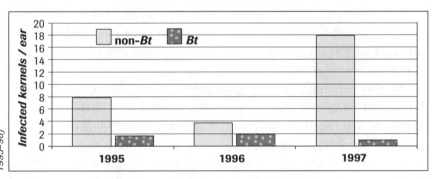

FIGURE 9A: Decrease in levels of fungal ear rot in *Bt* maize.

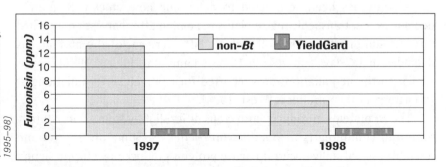

FIGURE 9B: Decrease in levels of mycotoxin (fumonisin) levels in *Bt* maize.

CHAPTER 3: FIRST GENERATION GM CROPS

How safe are *Bt*-protected crops? In 40 years of widespread use of *Bt* products (both the bacteria themselves and formulations of their insecticidal proteins), there have been no reports of adverse effects on human or animal health or on the environment (EPA, 1998). The Environmental Protection Agency (USA) has determined that the numerous toxicology studies conducted with *Bt* microbial products show no adverse effects. It has therefore concluded that these products are neither toxic nor pathogenic (McClintock *et al.*, 1995).

Enormous numbers of feeding trials have been carried out on rats, humans and mice (e.g. Noteborn *et al.*, 1994; Carter and Liggett, 1994; McClintock *et al.*, 1995; EPA Fact Sheet 1996). Based on accumulated data, the safety factor for human dietary exposure to *Bt* is greater than 50 000 for maize, greater than one million for potato and greater than two million for tomato. A safety factor is calculated by dividing the 'no-observed-effect-level' (NOEL) by the amount of *Bt* protein consumed. Both these amounts are measured in micrograms per kilogram of body weight per day. In plain language, what that means is that someone would have to consume 50 000 times more maize than normal in a day to observe any untoward effects! On the basis of these findings it is safe to conclude that *Bt* in crops is neither toxic nor pathogenic.

Another important point to remember is that the biological activity of different *Bt* proteins is highly specific. Noteborn *et al.* (1994) investigated *Bt* proteins and found no specific binding to mouse, rat, monkey or human gastrointestinal tract tissue. Furthermore, studies have shown that the gastric fluid can degrade more than 90% of *Bt* protein within 30 seconds in the human gastrointestinal tract.

A study has been conducted to determine how quickly *Bt* protein degrades when transgenic maize plants remaining after harvesting are tilled into the soil or left on the soil surface. Fifty per cent of the protein was degraded in 1.6 days and 90% in 15 days (Sims and Holden, 1996). This is similar to the degradation rates reported for commercial formulations of *Bt* bacteria or their products (West, 1984).

The *Bt* proteins introduced into crops differ slightly from their naturally occurring counterparts in *Bacillus thuringiensis*. Some are shorter and resemble the naturally occurring active proteins produced by enzyme action in the gastrointestinal tract of the insect (see Figure 7 on page 30). Others

34

may vary by a few amino acids. There is no reason to expect that these pose any unique human health concerns compared to their naturally occurring counterparts. Indeed, many of them have been found to be safe in the feeding trials mentioned above. A recent report by Betz *et al.* (2000) summarises the vast amount of safety data, both human and environmental, that has been published for both microbial *Bt* formulations and *Bt* crops.

The effect of *Bt* protein in pollen on the Monarch butterfly

Let us now consider the case of the butterfly that stamped (with apologies to Rudyard Kipling). In May 1999 scientists at Cornell University in the USA published a letter in the journal *Nature* (Losey *et al.*, 1999). In it they reported on a laboratory experiment in which they had placed monarch butterfly larvae on milkweed leaves covered with high levels of pollen from one particular *Bt* corn product. These larvae ate less, grew more slowly and suffered higher mortality rates than those placed on leaves covered with pollen from non-*Bt* corn. The authors stated that these effects were probably attributable to the *Bt* toxin in the pollen. They argued that this could threaten monarch butterflies (see Figure 10 on page 121 in the colour section), which feed on milkweed leaves, in the corn belt of the USA. This sparked a media frenzy with headlines such as the following from the *Daily Mail* in the United Kingdom: 'GM pollen that can mean a cloud of death for butterflies'.

In fact, the study did not tell scientists anything that they did not already know. The particular type of *Bt* gene used in the experiment produces a protein toxic to the European corn borer, whose larvae are similar to monarch butterfly larvae. Therefore it was obvious that if the latter consumed the toxin they would be killed. What was not clear from the study was how realistic the results were. Would there be sufficient *Bt* pollen on milkweed leaves in and around cornfields in America and Canada to pose a threat to monarch butterfly larvae? Do monarch butterfly larvae eat milkweed leaves covered with pollen? In fact, the same report showed that, given a choice, the larvae will avoid milkweed leaves covered with pollen, whether from *Bt* or non-*Bt* corn.

Since then field studies have been undertaken that tell a very different story from the above. Professor Mark Sears is Chair of the University of Guelph's Department of Environmental Biology in Canada. His research shows that pollen from Bt corn is not found in high enough doses on most milkweed plants to hurt monarch butterfly larvae (http://www.biotech-info.net). He examined milkweed stands within cornfields, at the edges of the fields and at distances of five, 10, 25, 50 and 100 metres away. Within the fields, he found pollen densities on milkweed leaves of approximately 150 grains per square centimetre. At the field edges, he found 80–100 grains per square centimetre, and at five metres, only one grain per square centimetre. He compared these findings to values obtained from a 'dose-response assay', which looked at the relationship between increasing doses of Bt pollen and mortality rates in monarch butterflies. The assay determined the dosages that would negatively affect monarch butterfly larvae. In the field, a dosage of 135 grains of Bt pollen per square centimetre of milkweed leaves had no greater effect on monarch larvae than similar amounts of non-Bt pollen. This dosage is fairly similar to pollen densities found within cornfields. This work was confirmed in published papers on 14 September 2001 (Sears *et al.*, Stanley-Horn *et al.*).

In another study a team of entomologists at the University of Nebraska tracked pollen shed and monarch butterfly activity around five *Bt* cornfields (M. Holmberg, Chemicals Editor, *Successful Farming*, personal communication, 2000/1). Most of the pollen remained within five metres of the fields and they found no corn pollen on milkweed plants further than 40 metres from the edge of the fields. There were no pollen counts above 20 grains per square centimetre on leaves more than five metres away from the field edge. Pollen densities less than 150 grains per square centimetre on milkweed leaves had no effect on monarch butterfly larvae. They found no dead monarch larvae on any milkweed leaves during the study. Again they showed that monarch butterfly larvae tend not to feed on milkweed leaves that carry any corn pollen, whether *Bt* or not.

These studies remind us of the central tenet of risk assessment: risk = hazard x exposure. Simply identifying a hazard, such as the potential to harm the monarch butterfly, is only one part of the equation. A real risk exists only when there is sufficient exposure to the hazard.

Public debate, however, started all over again when a supposed 'field study' by scientists in Ohio reported adverse effects on monarch butterfly larvae due to *Bt* pollen (Hansen Jesse and Obrycki, 2000). In their experiments they placed potted milkweeds at various distances from *Bt* corn crops and, in the laboratory, fed larvae on small discs cut from the leaves exposed in the field. Firstly, this experiment can hardly be described as a field study. Secondly, Hodgson (2000, p. 1030) points out that 'during 1999 more than 28 million acres [in the USA] were planted with Bt corn. In the same period, the monarch butterfly population flourished and increased by about 30% according to [the environmental monitoring group] Monarch Watch'.

A true field study by scientists from the University of Illinois found that *Bt* pollen is not toxic to black swallowtail butterflies (Wraight *et al.*, 2000). These butterflies are potentially at risk from this technology as their host plants survive mainly in narrow strips between roads and cornfields.

The story in summary…

- **Losey *et al.*:** Laboratory feeding studies show that *Bt* corn pollen on milkwood leaves affects monarch butterfly larvae adversely (1999)
- **Sears:** Pollen doses on milkweed leaves in the field are too low to harm monarch butterfly larvae (2000)
- **University of Nebraska:** Monarch butterfly larvae avoid pollen-coated leaves; pollen doses on milkweed leaves too low to harm larvae (2000/1)
- **Hansen Jesse and Obrycki:** Leaf segments from potted milkweeds harm larvae in laboratory tests (2000)
- **Wraight *et al.*:** *Bt* corn pollen is not toxic to black swallowtail butterfly larvae (2000)
- **Sears *et al.*, Stanley-Horn *et al.*:** Sears results confirmed (2001)

Gene flow from *Bt* crops to their wild relatives

The widespread planting of *Bt*-protected crops raises the question of the potential for the flow of the genes to wild plant species. This was thoroughly examined and addressed prior to the release of *Bt* potato, maize and cotton in the USA, Canada and in other countries where use is approved. In South Africa the South African Genetic Experimentation Committee (SAGENE) did similar assessments before allowing field trials and commercial release of *Bt* cotton and maize. Potatoes and cotton have no sexually compatible species in North America or South Africa. However, the potential for, and possible consequences of, gene flow to wild species will always be considered on a case-by-case basis. Mexico is the only country where out-crossing from maize to wild species could occur and their regulatory authorities are considering whether this could have a negative impact on the environment.

SAGENE: the South African Genetic Experimentation Committee. This body was responsible for reviewing applications for contained, trial and commercial releases of GMOs. It made recommendations to the relevant Ministry, until the implementation of the GMO Act in 2000.

Insect resistance to *Bt*

Pests exposed to *Bt*-protected crops can potentially develop resistance to these insecticidal proteins. Insecticide resistance would not be unique to Bt-expressing plants. Such resistance occurs repeatedly with conventional chemical insecticides and is also possible with *Bt* crops. Therefore, companies in the USA, in partnership with the regulatory authorities and academic scientists, have implemented aggressive resistance management plans to ensure the prolonged efficacy of *Bt*-protected crops.

The basis of this integrated pest management approach is that growers must plant sufficient acreage of non-*Bt* crops to serve as 'refuges' for pests. This decreases the selection pressure for the development of *Bt*-resistant insects and ensures that *Bt*-sensitive pests will be available as mates for *Bt*-resistant insects, should they develop. The offspring of these matings will be *Bt*-sensitive thus diminishing the spread of resistance in the insect population (Gould, 1998). The effectiveness of this approach is being monitored in the USA (e.g. Shelton *et al.*, 2000). To date, we have not observed any significant changes in insect sensitivity to *Bt* crops. In Africa it should be possible to use this system on commercial farms but it remains to be seen how effectively it can be managed among small-scale farmers. The authorities in charge of regulating the use of GM crops in these countries will have to pay particular attention to this.

Products are now entering the market containing two different *Bt* genes, which produce *Bt* proteins with different modes of action. The introduction of such products further reduces the likelihood that insect resistance will develop to a significant extent.

A relatively new approach to the problem of insect resistance was reported recently (Kota *et al.*, 1999). These scientists found that very high levels of expression of the *Bt* toxin could be obtained by introducing the *Bt* gene into **chloroplasts** rather than the nucleus. Each plant cell contains only one nucleus but many chloroplasts. Therefore if genes are introduced into chloroplast DNA, each cell will contain many copies, resulting in the production of high levels of *Bt* toxin. These high levels will be sufficient to kill insects, even if they have developed some resistance to *Bt*. There are other advantages to introducing transgenes into chloroplasts. These organelles are, with very few exceptions, only inherited maternally. In other words, they are not found in pollen. Therefore there is very little chance of the genes being transferred into non-target plants by cross-pollination, or of non-target insects being affected by toxins potentially present in pollen.

Chloroplast: an organelle found in a plant cell. It produces the chlorophyll pigment and is the site where photosynthesis occurs. In this process, carbon dioxide and water molecules are combined to form organic compounds using sunlight energy. Large numbers of chloroplasts are found in plant cells and they contain their own DNA.

Advantages of Bt *crops*

In conclusion, *Bt*-protected crops have demonstrated significantly improved yields and allowed a reduction in the use of chemical pesticides. This is leading to an increase in biodiversity of non-target insects and, possibly, also birds. The *Bt* proteins are not toxic to other animals or humans. However, the potential for the development of insect resistance to *Bt* needs to be carefully monitored.

Herbicide resistance

Weeds compete with crops for moisture, nutrients and light. Uncontrolled weed growth can thus result in significant losses in yield. Farmers have therefore been spraying herbicides on their crops for decades. As with insecticidal sprays, this is often done using aeroplanes, with the result that a great deal of the spray drifts away from the target sites.

The best-known example of transgenic herbicide resistance is Monsanto's **RoundupReady™ soybean.** The active ingredient in the herbicide **Roundup** is a compound called glyphosate. Glyphosate acts on an enzyme found in many plants, including soybeans and dicot weeds. Using Roundup as a weedkiller on soybean fields is a tricky business as the herbicide must not make contact with the crop but only with the weeds. Roundup Ready™ soybeans produce a naturally occurring form of the target enzyme that is naturally resistant to glyphosate and hence to the herbicide Roundup. Thus Roundup does not kill these soybeans but does kill the weeds.

Roundup Ready™ soybeans were introduced commercially in 1996. By 1999 they accounted for 54% of the total worldwide soybean acreage (James, 1999) and 58% by 2000 (James, 2000). Over 100 million acres of Roundup Ready™ soybeans have been grown to date, including approximately 95% of soybeans grown in Argentina. What has caused such large numbers of farmers to choose these herbicide-resistant soybeans?

Skeptics say that all the advantages of Roundup Ready™ soybeans accrue to Monsanto, as the company is now able to sell more of its herbicide than before. Monsanto claims that Roundup, a broad spectrum, biodegradable herbicide, is naturally broken down in the soil to innocuous products like ammonia, phosphate, carbon dioxide and water. It does not, like some other herbicides, accumulate in the environment or the food chain. Furthermore, it need only be used when weed control is required, which allows farmers to spend less on the weedkiller. Because the transformed soybean plants are resistant to the weedkiller, farmers can spray the crop at a precise time to kill emerging weeds without killing the crop. By the time the new weeds emerge, the crop has grown tall enough to starve them of light. The result is that less weedkiller is needed. Figure 11 shows that, between 1996 and 1999, there was an overall drop in herbicide use on soybeans in the USA of approximately 10%.

Roundup Ready™ soybeans: transgenic soybeans that produce a genetically modified version of the target enzyme that is resistant to Roundup.

Roundup: a herbicide that targets an enzyme found in many plants, including soybeans and dicot weeds.

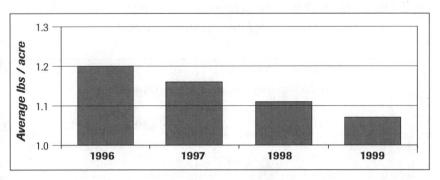

FIGURE 11: Reduction in the use of herbicide on soybeans in the USA since 1996. *(Source: Deane Market Research for conventional and Roundup Ready™ soybeans)*

However, there have been conflicting reports on the reduction in the use of herbicides since the introduction of Roundup Ready™ soybeans. Leonard Gianessi and Janet Carpenter used data from the United States Department of Agriculture and found that herbicide use, in terms of total pounds applied, rose 14% between 1995, the year before the introduction of the Roundup Ready™ soybeans, and 1998. This increase occurred while there was a 12% increase in acreage under soybeans, so overall, there has been a slight increase in herbicide use. However, it is difficult to conclude that this slight increase was due to an increase in herbicide use on Roundup Ready™ soybeans. Indeed Carpenter comments 'we would expect to see a much greater increase in total pounds of herbicide applied if [its] use on herbicide tolerant crops was greater than on conventional varieties' (22 May 2000; http://www.agbioworld.org).

What Gianessi and Carpenter did find was a large reduction in the *number* of herbicide applications made in 1998 compared to 1995. They calculated an aggregate reduction of 16 million herbicide applications over this period. This indicates that growers are able to use fewer active ingredients per acre and spray each field less often. As herbicide is often applied from aeroplanes, this means considerably less drift of herbicide from farms to the surrounding countryside. The Gianessi and Carpenter report can be found on http://www.ncfap.org/soy85.pdf and is consistent with data shown in Figure 12. The Economic Research Service of the United States Department of Agriculture has also published a report showing significantly fewer herbicide treatments on herbicide tolerant crops (http://www.ers.usda.gov/epubs/pdf/aer786/aer786.pdf).

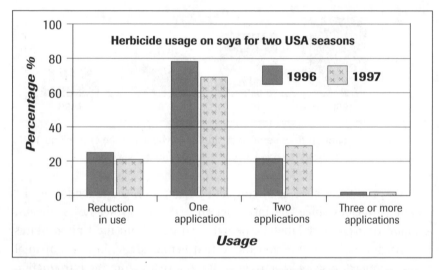

FIGURE 12: Percentage decrease in the number of herbicide applications to Roundup Ready™ soybeans. *(Source: Deane Market Research for conventional and Roundup Ready™ soybeans)*

In their most recent report, Gianessi and Carpenter (2001) estimated that soybean farmers in the USA who had planted Roundup Ready™ soybeans made 19 million fewer herbicide applications than growers of conventional soybeans. They also estimated that planting Roundup Ready™ soybeans resulted in net savings of $216 million in weed control.

One of the most interesting questions is who benefits from using Roundup Ready™ soybeans. Falck-Zepeda *et al.* (2000) estimated for the 1997 soybean season in the USA that, of the over $1 billion of total benefit attributed to Roundup Ready™ soybeans, 76% (more than $796 million) accrued to farmers. Seven per cent or $74 million went to the technology innovator and seed companies and consumers shared the remaining 17%.

Interestingly, the planting of herbicide-resistant soybeans has encouraged conservation tillage, resulting in a decrease in soil erosion in the USA. In fields planted with unmodified soybeans, farmers often till the soil about three weeks before planting, allowing weeds to come up. They then spray the fields with herbicide and let them lie fallow to allow the herbicide to degrade. During that period rain and wind can cause a loss of topsoil. On the other hand, farmers can plant herbicide-resistant soybean seeds with the first till and allow weeds and beans to grow up together. They give time for the weeds to develop good root growth, at which stage lower herbicide doses provide effective weed control. If the field is sprayed at this stage, the weeds die within about ten days, leaving rows of healthy soybean plants. The weed roots help to hold the soil.

Another herbicide-tolerant crop that has expanded rapidly is canola. Over 60% of the canola grown in Canada has been genetically modified to be resistant to herbicides. A recent report by the Canola Council of Canada (2001) noted that growers who planted herbicide-resistant canola eliminated over 6 000 tons of herbicide in the 2000 growing season.

Transfer of herbicide resistance from crops to weedy relatives

In 1998 a workshop was held in the USA to consider the possibility that transgenic plants, including those resistant to herbicides, could cross-pollinate with wild relatives and hence produce potentially harmful weeds (Information Systems in Biotechnology News Report, October 1999, http://www.isb.vt.ecu). It focused on crop species that have weedy relatives in North America such as *Brassica* species (oil seed rape and canola).

Cultivated transgenic *Brassica* will hybridise with a number of weedy species and therefore transfer of the introduced gene is possible. Studies have therefore been initiated to investigate the consequences of such transfer. For instance, will the weedy species become more invasive than they were before due to some selective advantage conferred by the transferred gene?

Crawley *et al.* (2001) published the results of a ten-year study initiated in multiple crops (maize, soybean, potato and canola) with different traits, including insect resistance and herbicide tolerance. They found that the crops containing these traits were no more competitive and survived no longer than plants grown from control seed. In fact, under non-tilled conditions, none of the plants survived longer than three years. At present it is possible to control such weeds with alternative herbicides, but scientists are looking for a longer-term solution. Bear in mind that conventionally bred herbicide-resistant varieties of *Brassica* and other crops already exist and that there is no evidence that the transfer of these genes to weedy relatives has had any deleterious environmental impacts.

Resistance to plant viruses

Plants, unlike animals, do not have an immune system. They are therefore at the mercy of plant-infecting viruses. In some years the cassava mosaic virus has destroyed almost the entire cassava crop in parts of Africa (see Figure 13 on page 121 in the colour section).

Most **plant viruses** contain RNA as their genetic material. This is packaged inside a coat which usually consists of many identical molecules of protein, hence the name coat protein. This is shown diagrammatically for the tobacco mosaic virus in Figure 14.

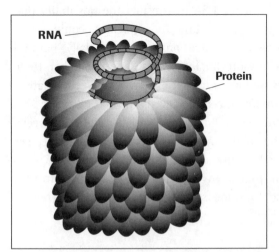

RNA

Protein

FIGURE 14: The structure of the tobacco mosaic virus showing RNA and coat protein molecules.

When such a virus infects a plant it must first 'uncoat' itself in order to replicate its RNA and synthesise more coat protein for its progeny. Scientists have found a way to prevent plant viruses replicating, thus developing virus-resistant plants. They have transformed plants with the viral gene that codes for its specific coat protein. These plants synthesise abundant amounts of coat protein. When the virus infects the cell, it becomes 'recoated' as fast as it tries to 'uncoat' itself. This 'coat protein mediated resistance' has been extremely efficient in developing potato plants resistant to potato viruses X and Y (Hackland *et al.*, 1994).

Only a small number of virus-resistant crops have been commercialised in the USA. However, Africa is host to a number of very virulent plant viruses. This topic will therefore be revisited in Chapter 10.

> **Plant virus:** an obligate parasite that consists of a core of DNA or RNA surrounded by a protein coat.

'Terminator Technology'

The last issue I will deal with in this chapter is the so-called 'Terminator Technology' developed by the United States Department of Agriculture in collaboration with the Delta and Pine Land seed company.

'Terminator Technology' was originally developed for two main reasons. The first was to prevent the spread of genes via pollen, a concern addressed earlier in this chapter. The second was to protect the 'proprietary property' developed by a seed company. Everybody understands the need for seed companies, like software manufacturers or record companies, to protect their property and investment in research and development. However, when this protection was applied to seeds, it threatened the ability of poor farmers to keep and plant their own seed. 'Terminator Technology' was received with a storm of objections.

How does this technology work? Put very simply, it means that the seeds of the genetically modified crop containing terminator genes will not grow unless the seed is specially treated. Thus, farmers who normally save seed produced during one growing season to plant the following year will be unable to do so. First world activists were quick to condemn this on

CHAPTER 3: FIRST GENERATION GM CROPS

behalf of third world farmers, fearing that the wealthy multinational seed companies would hold farmers in a stranglehold of dependency. However, this reaction reflects a simplistic understanding of farming practices in much of the developing world. It is true that small-scale farmers in some developing countries such as Mexico do save and plant their own seed. However, this is certainly not the case in much of sub-Saharan Africa.

Maize is the staple food of most of this region. Farmers know that if they plant their own seed the yield diminishes dramatically. This is because the best-yielding varieties of maize are hybrids. The farmer plants seeds resulting from a cross between two particular parent varieties developed especially to produce high quality seed. Farmers are very familiar with this so-called 'hybrid vigour'. These qualities are lost if the seed of the 'vigorous' plants are themselves planted. So most small-scale farmers in Africa currently buy seed every year. That is not to say they are totally dependent on hybrid seed. Over the years breeders have developed so-called 'open pollinated' varieties of maize. These produce reasonable yields and enable farmers to plant their own seed. But, not being the top producers, these varieties would never have the terminator gene introduced to them. Hence they would continue to be available to farmers worldwide.

Be that as it may, Monsanto has now yielded to public pressure and has put their 'Terminator Technology' on hold. However, there is one area in which it could play an invaluable role, and this is in the development of edible vaccines. I will discuss this and show the potentially valuable role of this technology in Chapter 10.

In summary ...

The first generation of genetically modified crops mainly benefit farmers and seed companies. They have, however, had a major positive impact on the environment, causing a decrease in the use of harmful chemical insecticides, increases in crop yields and a decrease in the numbers of times farmers need to spray their crops with herbicides.

References and further reading

Bennett, A. L., Bennett, A., Green, W., Du Toit, C. L. N., Richter, E., Van Staden, L., Brits, D., Friis, F. and Van Jaarsveld, J. (submitted) Bollworm control with transgenic (*Bt*) cotton. First results from Africa. *African Entomology*.

Betz, F. S., Hammond, B. G. and Fuchs, R. S. (2000) Safety and advantages of *Bacillus thuringiensis*-protected plants to control insect pests. *Regulatory Toxicology and Pharmacology*. Vol. 32, pp. 156–173.

Cahagnier, B. and Melcion, D. (2000) Mycotoxines de Fusarium dans les mais-grains a la recolte; relation entre la presence d'insectes (pyrale, sesamie) et la teneur en mycotoxines. In: Piva, G. and Masoero, F. (eds) *Proceedings of the Sixth International Feed Conference. Food Safety: current situation and perspectives in the European Community*. Piacenza, Italy, 27–28 November 2000. pp. 237–249.

Canola Council of Canada (2001) An agronomic and economic assessment of transgenic canola. Unpublished report, January 2001.

Carter, J. N. and Liggett, M. P. (1994) Acute oral toxicity and infectivity/pathogenicity to rats of EG 7841. Huntingdon Research Centre Ltd., Huntingdon, Cambridgeshire, England. HRC Study Report No. ECO 6/942538.

Crawley, M. J., Brown, S. L., Hails, R. S., Kohn, D. D. and Rees, M. (2001) Transgenic crops in natural habitats. *Nature*. Vol. 409, pp. 682–683.

Dogan, E. B., Berry, R. E., Reed, G. L. and Rossignol, P. A. (1996) Biological parameters of convergent lady beetle (Coleoptera; Coccinellidae) feeding on aphids (Homoptera; Aphidadae) on transgenic potato. *Journal of Economic Entomology*. Vol. 89, pp. 1105–1108.

Dowd, P. (2000) Indirect reduction of era molds and associated mycotoxins in *Bacillus thuringiensis* corn under controlled and open field conditions: utility and limitations. *Journal of Economic Entomology*. Vol. 93, pp. 1669–1679.

EPA Fact Sheet for *Bacillus thuringiensis* subspecies *kurstaki* Cry1Ac delta endotoxin and its controlling sequences as expressed in corn. December 20, 1996.

EPA. (1998) Registration eligibility decision: *Bacillus thuringiensis*. EPA 738-R-98-004, March 1998.

Falck-Zepeda, J. B., Traxler, G. and Nelson, R. G. (2000) Rent creation and distribution from biotechnology innovations: the case of *Bt* cotton and herbicide-tolerant soybeans in 1997. *Agribusiness*. Vol. 16, pp. 1–23.

Gianessi, L. P. and Carpenter, J. E. (1999) A*gricultural biotechnology: insect control benefits*. National Center for Food and Agricultural Policy, Washington.

Gianessi, L. P. and Carpenter, J. E. (2001) *Agricultural biotechnology: updated benefit estimates*. January 2001. National Center for Food and Agricultural Policy, Washington.

Gould, F. (1998) Sustainability of transgenic insecticidal cultivars: integrating pest genetics and ecology. *Annual Review of Entomology*. Vol. 43, pp. 701–726.

Hackland, A. F., Rybicki, E. P. and Thomson, J. A. (1994) Coat protein-mediated resistance in transgenic plants. *Archives of Virology.* Vol. 139, pp. 1–22.

Hansen Jesse, L. C. and Obrycki, J. J. (2000) Field deposition of *Bt* transgenic corn pollen: lethal effects on the monarch butterfly. *Oecologia.* Vol. 125, pp. 241–248.

Hodgson, J. (2000) Critics slam new Monarch *Bt* corn data criticised. *Nature Biotechnology.* Vol. 18, p. 1030.

James, C. (1997) Global status of transgenic crops in 1997. *ISAAA Briefs.* No. 5. ISAAA, Ithaca, N.Y.

James, C. (1998) Global review of commercialized transgenic crops: 1998. *ISAAA Briefs.* No. 8. ISAAA, Ithaca, N.Y.

James, C. (1999) Global review of commercialized transgenic crops: 1999. *ISAAA Briefs.* No. 12. ISAAA, Ithaca, N.Y.

James, C. (2000) Preview: global review of commercialized transgenic crops: 2000. *ISAAA Briefs.* No. 21. ISAAA, Ithaca, N.Y.

Kline and Company (2000) Plant biotech impact business analysis 2009. Unpublished report.

Klotz-Ingram, C., Jans, S., Fernandez-Cornejo, J. and McBride, W. (1999) Farm-level production effects related to the adoption of genetically modified cotton for pest management. *AgBioForum.* Vol. 2, pp. 73–84.

Kota, M., Daniell, H., Varma, S., Garczynski, S. F., Gould, F. and Moar, W. J. (1999) Overexpression of *Bacillus thuringiensis* (*Bt*) CryA2Aa2 protein in chloroplasts confers resistance to plants against susceptible and *Bt*-resistant insects. *Proceedings of the National Academy of Sciences,* USA. Vol. 96, pp.1840–1845.

Losey, J. E., Rayor, L. S. and Carter, M. E. (1999) Transgenic pollen harms monarch larvae. *Nature.* Vol. 399, p. 214.

McClintock, J. T., Schaffer, C. R. and Sjoblad, R. D. (1995) A comparative review of the mammalian toxicity of *Bacillus thuringiensis*-based pesticides. *Pesticide Science.* Vol. 45, pp. 95–105.

Marasas, W. F. O., Jaskiewicz, K., Venter, F. S. and Van Schalkwyk, D. J. (1988) *Fusarium moniliforme* contamination of maize in oesophageal cancer areas in the Transkei. *South African Medical Journal.* Vol. 74, pp. 110–114.

Monsanto. (1999) Ingard cotton: research and performance review 1998–1999.

Munkvold, G. P., Hellmich, R. L. and Showers, W. B. (1997) Reduced Fusarium ear rot and symptomless infection in kernels of maize genetically engineered for European corn borer resistance. *Phytopathology.* Vol. 87, pp. 1071–1077.

Munkvold, G. P., Hellmich, R. L. and Rice, L. R. (1999) Comparison of fumonisin concentrations in kernels of transgenic *Bt* maize hybrids and nontransgenic hybrids. *Plant Disease.* Vol. 83, pp. 130–138.

Norred, W. P. (1993) Fumonisins – mycotoxins produced. *Journal of Toxicology and Environmental Health.* Vol. 38, pp. 309–328.

Noteborn, H. P. J. M., Rienenmann-Ploum, M. E., Van den Berg, J. H. J., Alink, G. M., Zolla, L. and Kuiper, H. A. (1994) Consuming transgenic food crops: the toxicological and safety aspects of tomato expressing Cry1Ab and NPTII. ECB6. *Proceedings of the Sixth European Congress on Biotechnology.* Elsevier Science, Amsterdam.

Oberhauser, Karen S. *et al.* (2001) Temporal and spacial overlap between monarch larvae and corn pollen, *PNAS Online*, September.

Pietri, A. and Piva, G. (2000) Occurrence and control of mycotoxins in maize grown in Italy. In: Piva, G. and Masoero, F. (eds) *Proceedings of the Sixth International Feed Conference. Food Safety: current situation and perspectives in the European Community.* Piacenza, Italy, 27–28 November 2000. pp. 226–236.

Pleasants, John, M *et al.* (2001) Corn pollen deposition on milkweeds in and near cornfields, *PNAS Online*, September.

Sears, Mark K. *et al.* (2001) Impact of *Bt* corn pollen on monarch butterfly populations: A risk assessment. *PNAS Online*, September.

Shelton, A. M., Tang, J. D., Roush, R. T., Metz, T. D. and Earle, E. D. (2000) Field tests on managing resistance to *Bt*-engineered plants. *Nature Biotechnology.* Vol. 18, pp. 339–342.

Sims, S. R. and Holden, L. R. (1996) Insect bioassay for determining soil degradation of *Bacillus thuringiensis* subsp. *kurstaki* CrylA(b) protein in corn tissues. *Physiological Chemistry and Ecology.* Vol. 25, pp. 659–664.

Smith, R. (1999) Alabama entomologist believes genetic engineering and eradication will usher in new era of cotton pests. *Cotton Grower Plus.* March 1999, p. 18.

Stanley-Horn, Diane E. *et al* (2001) Assessing the impact of Cry1Ab-expressing corn pollen on monarch butterfly larvae in field studies. *PNAS Online*, September.

Traxler, G. and Falck-Zepeda, J. (1999) The distribution of benefits from the introduction of transgenic cotton varieties. *AgBioForum.* Vol. 2, pp. 94–98.

Wraight, C. L., Zangerl, A. R., Carroll, M. J. and Berenbaum, M. R. (2000) Absence of toxicity of *Bacillus thuringiensis* pollen to black swallowtails under field conditions. *Proceedings of the National Academy of Sciences, USA.* Vol. 97, pp. 7700–7703.

West, A. W. (1984) Fate of the insecticidal, proteinaceous parasporal crystal of *Bacillus thuringiensis* in soil. *Soil Biology and Biochemistry.* Vol. 16, pp. 357–360.

Xia, J. Y., Cui, J. J., Ma, L. H., Dong, S. X. and Cui, X. F. (1999) The role of *Bt* cotton in integrated insect pest management. *Acta Gossypii Sinica.* Vol. 11, pp. 57–64.

Chapter 4

What's in it for the consumer?

Second generation GM crops

Golden rice

Whereas first generation GM crops primarily benefit seed companies and farmers, second generation crops are more likely to have direct benefits for consumers. One of the most exciting advances in GM crops so far has been the development of 'golden rice'. This rice provides consumers with both vitamin A and iron.

Vitamin A deficiency is a global problem. According to the World Health Organisation (WHO), 250 million children are at risk annually, and vitamin A deficiency is responsible for significant illness and death in about 10 million people. This deficiency results in impaired vision, reduced immune function and protein malnutrition (vitamin A affects the absorption and use of amino acids). A diet of rice can exacerbate iron deficiency, which is the primary micronutrient shortage. It afflicts up to 3.7 billion people, particularly women, leaving them weakened by anaemia and susceptible to complications during childbirth (Gura, 1999).

The best source of vitamin A are the **carotenes**, particularly *ß*-carotene, found in many fruits and vegetables. The body converts carotenes into vitamin A and it is generally accepted that it is safer to consume carotenes than vitamin A itself. Fruits and vegetables with high carotene contents, such as mangoes, spinach, carrots and pumpkins, are not routinely available at affordable prices to poor people in Africa and Asia, particularly in urban areas. Fortification of crops that can be grown by small-scale farmers on these continents could do much to alleviate vitamin A deficiencies.

In order to address the problem of vitamin A deficiency, scientists at the Swiss Federal Institute of Technology, funded by the Rockefeller Foundation, have inserted genes from the daffodil and other plants producing carotene into rice. The grains of this transgenic rice are a light golden-yellow in colour and contain sufficient β-carotene to meet human vitamin A requirements.

The scientists inserted two further genes into golden rice to make it a good source of iron. Firstly, a gene from a French bean boosts its iron content. The other gene produces an enzyme that counteracts the effect of phytic acid, a substance found in rice that inhibits the body's ability to absorb iron. The proteins produced by these genes are stable even after cooking, making golden rice a real winner for the approximately 2.4 billion people who eat rice as their staple diet.

On 16 May 2000 a collaboration was announced that will hopefully bring golden rice to the people of Asia by 2003. The inventors, Ingo Potrykus and Peter Beyer, reached an agreement with Greenovation, a small biotechnology company linked to a German university, and the seed company, Zeneca. This agreement will make this technology available free of charge for humanitarian purposes in the developing world. Gary Toenniessen, Director of Food Security at the Rockefeller Foundation, endorsed the agreement, saying, 'this collaboration will speed the process of conducting all appropriate nutritional and safety testing and obtaining regulatory approvals. The agreement should help assure that golden rice reaches those people it can help most as quickly as possible. We look forward to following the progress of this agreement as a possible model for other public–private partnerships designed to benefit poor people in developing countries' (17 May 2000, AgBioView@listbot.com).

In terms of the deal, Zeneca buys commercial rights to golden rice from Greenovation, which acts as intermediary for the inventors. Zeneca then licenses 'non-commercial' rights back to the inventors and undertakes to help them improve the grain, deal with patenting issues and guide golden rice through the costly testing and regulatory process. The inventors will distribute the rice free of charge to government-run plant breeding centres and agricultural institutes in China, India and other rice-dependent Asian nations. Local farmers will each be allowed to earn $10 000 per annum without having to pay royalties. In exchange, Zeneca will commercialise golden rice in the developed world as one of a range of 'functional foods' which analysts believe are poised to revolutionise eating habits among an increasingly health-conscious population.

Critics of the use of GM crops say that there are better ways of alleviating these nutritional deficiencies, such as building roads to facilitate the distribution of vitamin pills and iron supplements. But it would cost trillions of dollars to build good roads in flood-prone places like Bangladesh and mountainous countries like Nepal. Handing out pills is simple and cheap if you can get them to remote villages and if people understand the importance of taking them every day. India's Vandana Shiva, a tireless crusader against GM crops, says that better alternatives are liver, egg yolk, chicken, meat and leafy vegetables (Shiva, 2001). Like a modern-day Marie Antoinette, she seems to say, 'Let them eat chicken!'

Vitamin A: also called retinol; a vitamin essential for growth and vision in dim light; found in green and yellow vegetables, egg yolk and fish-liver oil.

Carotene: an orange or red plant pigment that is a precursor of vitamin A.

Food for healthy hearts

While the example of golden rice illustrates the power of biotechnology to address a well-established dietary deficiency, the same technology can also be harnessed to address the nutritional needs of most advanced countries of the world by producing new nutrients. As our understanding of the human genome, diseases and degenerative process increases, we are likely to uncover the role of many nutrients that can accelerate or inhibit such processes. We can then use biotechnology to eliminate potentially harmful compounds or increase the levels of beneficial ones in order to help us live healthier lives.

One example of a potentially harmful compound is cholesterol. Cardiovascular disease, linked to high levels of dietary cholesterol, is becoming ever more prevalent, both in the Western world and in Africa. While people with very high cholesterol levels are prescribed drugs, these are expensive and not recommended for people with intermediate levels of blood cholesterol. Very few people with intermediate levels of cholesterol follow the recommended practice of reducing their saturated fat intake and taking regular exercise. We have known for some time that plant sterols (**phytosterols**) can reduce cholesterol in humans by 10–15% by interfering with cholesterol absorption in the gastrointestinal tract. Plant sterols are not currently available in adequate quantities in the foods we eat and scientists are actively engaged in increasing the phytosterol content of several grains (Kishore and Shewmaker, 1999).

Vegetable oils are another example of how genetic engineering can improve the quality of a food product. Canola and soybeans, the source of most of the cooking oil in the Western world, often contain 'trans-fatty acids', substances that may increase the risks of heart disease. GM varieties that are free of these trans-fatty acids are now being evaluated for commercial viability. Furthermore, unsaturated fatty acids are healthier than saturated fatty acids. **Oleic acid** and **linoleic acid** are both unsaturated fatty acids. Oleic acid is more stable in frying and cooking than linoleic acid. Scientists have succeeded in increasing oleic acid concentrations in the seeds of genetically modified varieties from 25% to 85% (see Mazur *et al.*, 1999).

Table 1 on the next page compares the compositions of various oils currently being developed by the introduction of mutations or by genetic engineering. These are all variants of canola, which was itself selected as a variant form of oil-seed rape (*Brassica napus*).

Phytosterols: sterols produced by plants, some of which are able to reduce cholesterol in humans.

Linoleic acid: an unsaturated fatty acid that is not stable in frying and cooking.

Oleic acid: an unsaturated fatty acid that is stable in frying and cooking.

Oil type	Method used	Fatty acid composition in %				In use
		Saturated fats	Oleic acid	Linoleic acid	Linolenic acid	
Canola	Selection	7	**61**	21	9	Yes
Low linolenic	Mutations	7	63	25	**<2**	Yes
High oleic/ Low linolenic	Mutation	7	**76**	15	**2**	Yes
High linoleic	Genetic modification[a]	7	57	**28**	6	No
High oleic	Genetic modification[b]	7	**84**	5	3	No
Low saturated fats	Genetic modification[c]	**3**	66	21	**10**	No
Low saturated fats/high oleic	Genetic modification[d]	**3**	**90**	5	3	No

TABLE 1: Existing and future changes to the compositions of fatty acids in canola oil derivatives. The numbers in bold indicate favourable levels.

a   Developed by DuPont.
b   Developed by DuPont: gene only active in the embryo where oil is produced.
c   Developed by Calgene: Any oil with less than 7% saturated fats can be labeled in the USA as containing low saturated fats.
d   Still in the development stages.

(Source: Downey and Taylor, 1996)

More improved food and fodder

Other second generation GM crops include high-lysine maize and soybean for improved animal feed. Lysine is an essential amino acid that is present at very low levels in maize- and soy-based animal feeds. Conventional feeds therefore have to be supplemented with lysine. High-lysine maize and soybean varieties are currently in the testing stages (see Mazur *et al.*, 1999).

Scientists have altered the composition of potatoes to increase their starch content by up to 20%. This increase does not affect potatoes if they are baked or boiled but is advantageous when they are fried. High starch potatoes contain less water. During the frying process water is replaced by oil and therefore the high starch potatoes absorb less oil. The resulting 'French fries' are more nutritious and healthier due to the decrease in oil content. They also fry more quickly, which is an advantage in the fast food industry (Stark, 1992).

Phytoestrogens are oestrogens found in plants. They are currently generating a great deal of attention because of their potential health benefits. There is evidence that they reduce the risk of osteoporosis, decrease cholesterol levels and slow the development of hormone-related cancers. Therapeutic phytoestrogens, such as isoflavones, are currently selling in the form of over-the-counter soybean extract pills. However, not all plants produce sufficient levels of isoflavones and processing can account for losses of up to 50%. Therefore scientists are using genetic modification to produce a more reliable and uniform source of this valuable phytoestrogen (Shmaefsky, 2000).

Oestrogen: a hormone that produces changes in the female sexual organs.

Phytoestrogen: oestrogen produced by plants.

The Flavr Savr™ tomato

A good example of genetic modification to improve food quality is the Flavr Savr™ tomato, which came onto the market in the USA in 1994 (see Figure 15 on page 122 of the colour section). It was the first genetically modified fresh fruit or vegetable to reach the market. Commercially available tomatoes often have very little flavour because they are picked too early. This is because they need to be transported, delivered to markets and sold before they get soft and start to rot. Farmers therefore pick them while they are green but before they can absorb the flavour-enhancing compounds from the parent vine. They may look great but they often taste like cardboard!

If the ripening process could be slowed down, tomatoes could be left on the vine longer, still look good on supermarket shelves but taste much better. Hence the genetically modified tomato was called 'Flavr Savr'. One of the genes involved in the ripening process produces an enzyme called pectinase that breaks down the pectin in tomatoes. This compound found in the walls of plant cells gives the tomato its firmness. As it breaks down the tomato ripens and softens.

Scientists at Calgene slowed down the ripening process by decreasing the rate at which the gene produces pectinase (Redenbaugh *et al., 1992*). They did this using so-called 'antisense RNA technology', shown diagrammatically in Figure 16. They inserted the ripening gene into tomato DNA in the opposite orientation to the normal ripening gene. When the inserted gene is transcribed, it forms an RNA molecule that is complementary to the RNA produced by the normal ripening gene. The two RNA molecules combine and therefore less RNA is available to be translated into ripening protein. This slows the rate of production of ripening protein.

It is estimated that up to half the fruit and vegetables grown commercially are lost to spoilage. Research groups are aiming to produce a range of other slow-ripening fruits and vegetables with a longer storage life to reduce wastage.

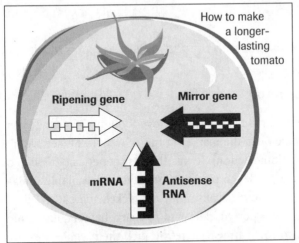

FIGURE 16: Antisense RNA slows down the ripening process. The plant produces a piece of RNA complementary to the RNA produced by the ripening gene. The two strands of RNA combine to form a complex. This slows down, but does not prevent, RNA from the ripening gene being translated into the ripening protein.

Another advantage of the tomatoes with delayed ripening properties is that they have a lower water content. The higher ratio of solid to water in GM tomatoes makes them produce better pastes and ketchup. The company Zeneca in the United Kingdom used a different approach to Calgene to produce a tomato with similar properties (Sanders *et al.*, 1998). Tomato puree from these tomatoes appeared on supermarket shelves in the United Kingdom in 1996. Interestingly, they were labeled as being derived from genetically modified tomatoes but, being cheaper and somewhat better flavoured, they outsold their conventional counterparts. It was only in 1998, when the furore against GM foods erupted in the United Kingdom, that sales declined and they were ultimately removed from supermarket shelves.

Fish genes in tomatoes?

A group from the company DNAP (DNA Plant Technology) from Oakland, California, published a paper in 1991 in which they described the introduction into tomatoes of an 'antifreeze' gene from an Arctic flounder (Hightower *et al.*, 1991). This came to the attention of the media some years later and caused an uproar, with headlines implying that a single gene from a fish could render a tomato no longer a vegetable. Newspaper cartoonists had a field day with fish/tomato hybrids. Indeed one of the symbols used for the 'Five Year Freeze' campaign in the United Kingdom is a half tomato-half fish monster. The actual story is that the experiment did not work. The antifreeze protein had no effect on the tomatoes whatever: if put into the freezer and then thawed out they were still as 'squishy' as their untransformed counterparts. The company abandoned the project. It would be good if the media did so as well.

Micronutrients

Humans require a diverse, well-balanced diet containing a complex mixture of both macronutrients and micronutrients in order to maintain optimal health. Macronutrients include carbohydrates, lipids and proteins. They make up the bulk of the food we eat and are used primarily as an energy supply. Micronutrients are organic and inorganic compounds present in small amounts and are not used for energy. Essential micronutrients include 17 minerals and 13 vitamins. While the majority of people at risk of micronutrient deficiencies are in the developing world, even in industrialised nations deficiencies are surprisingly common due to poor eating habits (DellaPenna, 1999). Table 2 gives examples of health-promoting micronutrients found in plants. Scientists are trying to find ways of delivering these and other valuable compounds to a wider range of people at risk for deficiencies.

Plant chemical	Disease ameliorated or prevented	Active compound and plant source
Carotenoids	Prostate, oesophageal and other cancers; cardiovascular disease; macular degeneration	Lycopene: tomatoes Lutein: kale, spinach
Glucosinolates	Cancers	Glucoraphanin: broccoli
Phytoestrogens	Cardiovascular disease; osteoporosis; breast, prostate and colon cancers	Genistein and deidzein: soybeans
Phenolics	Cardiovascular disease; cancers	Resveratrol: red grapes

TABLE 2: Examples of micronutrients found in plants. *(Source: DellaPenna, 1999)*

Metals and minerals

Metals like aluminium, the earth's most abundant metal, can be enemies of plant growth. Normally aluminium is locked up in mineral compounds and in this form it is not dangerous to plants. However, in many parts of Africa, soils are acidic and this low pH liberates aluminium ions that can poison plant roots. The result is stunted growth and poor harvests. Plant breeders have coped with this problem by crossing metal-sensitive plant varieties with the few species that can thrive in soil containing aluminium ions. Unfortunately, such varieties are few and classical breeding is slow. Recently, however, several research groups have identified metal-resistance genes. Some allow plants to thrive in soils containing four times the level of aluminium that stunts the growth of normal plants.

Plants containing these genes could also be used in environmental remediation. If these plants were grown in soils contaminated with metals, they would absorb the metals and could then be harvested and deposited in landfill sites. It has been estimated that the cost of using plants to clean up polluted soils could be less than one-tenth the cost of making it into concrete or digging up the soil and transporting it to a hazardous waste landfill site. Plants are already being used to clean up mercury, a lethal waste product found at various industrial sites. A bacterial gene has been introduced into a number of plant species, including canola, tobacco and poplar. The gene allows these plants to grow on mercury-laden media and release the metal into the air. While some might cringe at the thought of plants emitting trails of mercury vapour, scientists argue that, compared to the existing concentration of mercury in the air, plants growing on contaminated sites would merely add trace amounts (Moffat, 1999a).

Another environmentally friendly use of GM plants is the production of protein-based, biodegradable polymers to replace decidedly environmentally unfriendly petroleum-based plastics. A number of reports have shown the possibility of producing such thermoplastic polymers in plants (e.g. Mittendorf *et al.*, 1998; Slater *et al.*, 1999). These natural polymers become plastic on heating and harden on cooling.

What's in the pipeline?

Taking a look into the future, it is interesting to note what GM crops are currently being tested and what is in the pipeline for future testing. Traits under investigation include:

- delayed fruit ripening and consequent improvements in flavour;
- improved nutritional quality, such as better amino acid and β-carotene content;
- extended flower life for horticulturally important plants;
- altered fatty acid composition for improved health, e.g. reducing heart disease;
- improved plant fibre quality and strength;
- decreased post-harvest toxin production due to fungal infection,
- resistance to worms;
- the ability of plants to fix nitrogen from the air, thus no longer requiring nitrogen fertilisers;
- tolerance to stresses such as high salinity, poor soil conditions and drought;
- improved photosynthesis to increase grain yield.

Table 3 lists some of the traits that are being developed that could be of great benefit to developing countries.

Traits currently in greenhouse or field tests	Traits currently in laboratory tests
Input traits	
■ Resistance to insects, worms, viruses, bacteria and fungi in crops such as rice, maize, potatoes, papaya and sweet potatoes ■ Delayed senescence, dwarfing and early flowering in rice ■ Tolerance of aluminium, submergence, chilling, and freezing in cereals ■ Male sterility to enable hybrid seed production in rice, maize, oil-seed rape and wheat ■ Increased yield potential in rice	■ Drought and salinity tolerance in cereals ■ Seedling vigour in rice ■ Enhanced phosphorus and nitrogen uptake in rice and maize ■ Resistance to the parasitic weed *Striga* in maize, rice and sorghum, to viruses in cassava and bananas, and to bacterial blight in cassava ■ Resistance to nematodes and to black sigatoka disease in bananas ■ Rice with alternative C_4 photosynthetic pathways and the ability to carry out nitrogen fixation
Output traits	
■ Increased ß-carotene in rice and oil-seed rape ■ Lower phytates in maize and rice to increase bio-available iron ■ Modified starch in rice, potato and maize and modified fatty acid content in oil-seed rape ■ Increased bio-available protein, essential amino acids, seed weight and sugar content in maize ■ Lowered lignin content of forage crops	■ Increased ß-carotene, delayed post-harvest deterioration and reduced content of toxic cyanides in cassava ■ Increased vitamin E in rice ■ Asexual seed production in maize, rice, millet and cassava ■ Delayed ripening in bananas ■ Use of genetically engineered plants such as potatoes and bananas as vehicles for production and delivery of recombinant vaccines to humans ■ Improved amino acid content of forage crops

TABLE 3: Biotechnology research relevant to developing countries. *(Source: Conway and Toenniessen, 1999)*

Edible vaccines

In developing countries, where the expense of needles and cold storage are prohibitive, edible vaccines could be a real boon for combating disease. Such vaccines are merely one aspect of what is covered by the term 'farmaceuticals', the use of plants as factories to produce therapeutic proteins.

Transgenic plants are very attractive for large-scale production of pharmaceutically important proteins. A crop such as tobacco needs little maintenance and is relatively cheap to grow. There is also a certain ironic satisfaction in the thought of producing anti-cancer drugs in tobacco plants! An additional advantage of producing pharmaceuticals using plants is the reduced risk of contamination by viruses that affect humans, such as human immunodeficiency virus (HIV) and hepatitis. These viruses can contaminate vaccines produced using animal hosts. The real advantages of edible vaccines are likely to be felt in the developing world and I will deal with this topic in greater detail in Chapter 11.

One of the challenges facing the general field of 'farmaceuticals' is the need to produce sufficiently high levels of a particular therapeutic protein. Recently Staub *et al.* (2000) managed to produce high concentrations of human somatotropin, used to treat dwarfism in children. By introducing the gene into choloroplast DNA, they produced somatotropin at levels greater than 7% of total protein, which was 300 times greater than when the gene was introduced into nuclear DNA.

An alternative to edible vaccines is to produce vaccines in tobacco plants. A number of scientists at the University of Cape Town are working on producing vaccines against HIV and against a virus that causes genital cancer in African women. This type of 'pharming' has a number of attractive features:

- Tobacco is a cheap, hardy crop and is easy to grow, even in poor soil.
- We can obtain relatively high yields of foreign proteins from transgenic tobacco, in the order of 100 milligrams per kilogram of leaf. These yields could be further increased if the protein is made in the chloroplasts, as described above.
- There is no risk that vaccines produced in tobacco will be contaminated by animal viruses that could potentially harm humans.

Potatoes in Peru

An interesting exercise that could benefit subsistence farmers in the Andes is being undertaken at the International Potato Centre (CIP) in Lima, Peru (Moffat, 1999b). The Andean region of Peru, Bolivia and Ecuador is the ancestral home of the potato, one of the developed world's favourite vegetables. Many Andean potatoes contain natural bitter compounds called glyco-alkaloids. The processing methods used to remove these also remove nutritious proteins and vitamins. Scientists at CIP have reduced glyco-alkaloid levels by about 40% in preliminary field tests and by 60% in greenhouse tests. Potato growers in the developed world could benefit from these GM approaches and the low glyco-alkaloid potatoes. Many of the primitive Andean potatoes have useful traits such as disease- and frost-resistance. However, due to their high glyco-alkaloid contents they have not been used in breeding programmes. That could all change thanks to genetic engineering.

In summary ...

There is no doubt that there are exciting GM crops in the pipeline. Many of them will be of greater benefit to the developing world than to industrialised nations. Hopefully the anti-GMO movements in Europe and elsewhere will not prevent their development, thus making them unavailable to these developing nations.

References and further reading

Conway, G. and Toenniessen, G. (1999) Feeding the world in the twenty-first century. *Nature*. Vol. 402, pp. C55–58.

DellaPenna, D. (1999) Nutritional genomics: manipulating plant micronutrients to improve human health. *Science*. Vol. 285, pp. 375–379.

Downey, R. K. and Taylor, D. C. (1996) Diversification of canola/rapeseed fatty acid supply for the year 2000. *Oleagineaux Corps gras Lipides*. Vol. 3, pp. 9–13.

Gura, T. (1999) New genes boost rice nutrients. *Science*. Vol. 285, pp. 994–995.

Hightower, R., Baden, C., Penzes, E., Lund P. and Dunsmuir, P. (1991) Expression of antifreeze proteins in transgenic plants. *Plant Molecular Biology.* Vol. 17, pp. 1013–1021.

Kishore, G. M. and Shewmaker, C. (1999) Biotechnology: enhancing human nutrition in developing and developed worlds. *Proceedings of the National Academy of Sciences,* USA. Vol. 96, pp. 5968–5972.

Mazur, B., Krebbers, E. and Tingey, S. (1999) Gene discovery and product development for grain quality traits. *Science.* Vol. 285, pp. 372–375.

Mittendorf, V., Robertson, E. J., Leech, R. M., Krüger, N., Steinbüchel, A. and Poirier, Y. (1998) Synthesis of medium chain-length polyhydroxyalkanoates in *Arabidopsis thaliana* using intermediates of peroxisomal fatty acid ß-oxidation. *Proceedings of the National Academy of Sciences, USA.* Vol. 95, pp. 369–370.

Moffat, A. S. (1999a) Engineering plants to cope with metals. *Science.* Vol. 285, pp. 369–370.

Moffat, A. S. (1999b) Crop engineering goes South. *Science.* Vol. 285, pp. 370–371.

Shiva, V. (2001) Genetically engineered 'Vitamin A Rice': a blind approach to blindness prevention. In: Tokar, B. (ed.) *Redesigning Life?* Zed Books, New York.

Redenbaugh, K., Hiatt, W. and Martineau, B. (1992) *Safety assessment of genetically engineered fruits and vegetables. A case study of the Flavr Savr tomato.* CRC Press Inc., Boca Raton.

Sanders, P. R., Lee, T. C., Groth, M. E., Astwood, J. D. and Fuchs, R. L. (1998) Safety assessment of insect-protected corn. In: Thomas, J. A. (ed) *Biotechnology and Safety Assessments.* Second Edition. Taylor and Francis, San Diego, Ca., pp. 241–256.

Shmaefsky, B. (2000) Boosting phytoestrogens a boon for people and plants. *Information Systems in Biotechnology (ISB) News Report.* April 2000.

Slater, S., Mitsky, T. A., Houmiel, K. L., Hao, M., Reiser, S. E. Taylor, N. B., Tran, M., Valentin, H. E., Rodriguez, D. J., Stone, D. A., Padgette, S. R., Kishore, G. and Grys, K. J. (1999) High yield production of a human therapeutic protein in tobacco chloroplasts. *Nature Biotechnology.* Vol. 17, pp. 1011–1016.

Stark, D.M (1992) Regulation of the amount of starch in plant tissues by ADP glucose pyrophosphorylase. *Science.* Vol. 258, pp. 287–292.

Staub, J. M., Garcia, B., Graves, J., Hajdukiewicz, P. T. J., Hunter, P., Nehra, N., Paradkar, V., Schlittler, M., Carroll, J. A., Spatola, L., Ward, D., Ye, G. and Russell, D. A. (2000) Metabolic engineering of *Arabidopsis* and *Brassica* for poly (3-hydroxybutyrate-co-3-hydroxyralerate) copolymer production. *Nature Biotechnology.* Vol. 18, pp. 333–338.

World Health Organisation (WHO). (1995) Global prevalence of vitamin A deficiency. *Micronutrient Deficiency Information Systems Working Paper No. 2.* WHO, Geneva.

Chapter 5

Cost-benefit analysis – is it worth it?

Trial by media

In August 1998 Arpad Pusztai, a scientist working at the Rowett Research Institute in Scotland, stirred up a media frenzy by announcing on television that data from his experiments showed that transgenic potatoes, carrying a lectin gene from snowdrops, were toxic to mice (*The Economist*, 20 February 1999, pp. 93–95). Lectins can be natural insecticides and some people thought that transferring the gene to potato plants might make them resistant to aphids. The Rowett Institute set up an investigatory committee to study the data. They came to the conclusion that the research methodology was flawed and that the data were, therefore, difficult to interpret.

However, it is important to understand the purpose of those experiments. A statement issued by the Rowett Research Institute on 12 February 1999 said, 'Dr Pusztai's studies did not involve the testing of foods about to be released onto the market. They were designed to explore whether we could develop more sensitive tests [to detect] any possible effect of different lectins on the intestine, should lectins be used in genetically manipulated crops.' In other words, the institute was considering using lectins as protective agents against insect pests in potatoes but they first wanted to develop sensitive tests to determine the potential toxicity of these lectins to animals and humans.

We know that certain lectins are toxic to insects and that transgenic plants carrying these genes might be resistant to insect pests. However, we also know that certain lectins may be toxic to and cause other adverse effects in animals. The tests were therefore designed to determine whether potatoes carrying this particular lectin might be toxic to animals. If they were, the project would not be pursued. Pusztai failed to make this connection in his media briefing and the subsequent public debate also failed to alert the public to this fact. Media coverage was hysterical and eventually the Royal Society stepped in to make an independent assessment of the data. The main conclusions of this assessment were as follows:

- Pusztai's work was flawed in many aspects of its design, execution and analysis and was therefore inconclusive. For instance, the lectin-containing potato had significant unintended changes in protein content. Consequently, the diets prepared with the GM potato and unmodified potato were not balanced, which is an essential prerequisite for a valid animal study. In addition, Pusztai changed the structure of the experiments as they progressed, which made it difficult to compare effects on the rats fed on GM potatoes and those fed on unmodified potatoes. Furthermore, he did not conduct the measurements 'blind' as is normal practice for trials of this kind. Unconscious bias is a well-known source of invalid results, so scientists and technicians involved in these experiments should not have known which rats were being fed GM or non-GM potatoes.

- There was no convincing evidence of adverse effects from GM potatoes. The data seemed to show slight differences between rats fed predominantly on GM or non-GM potatoes. However, technical limitations of the experiments and the incorrect use of statistical tests made it impossible to interpret the differences. (Remember also the point raised above: had the transgenic potatoes proved to be toxic, the Rowett Research Institute would have abandoned this line of insect resistance for safety reasons.)

- The Rowett Research Institute used only one method to insert a single gene to modify a particular product from one species of animal. However skillful the experiments, we cannot justify drawing general conclusions about whether GM foods are harmful to humans or not based on this one experiment. We must assess each GM food individually.

This whole episode underlines how important it is for research scientists to share their results with other scientists who are able to offer informed criticism before releasing them into the public arena. In other words, scientific disclosure by media exposure *prior* to publication is highly suspect. If a scientist is not prepared to subject her or his data to scientific scrutiny, but instead chooses to go directly to the media, the public ought to be extremely skeptical as to the accuracy of those data.

This case illustrates the importance of analysing GM crops on a case-by-case basis to determine whether there are any risks attached and whether the benefits outweigh these. We do not live in a risk-free world. We do not know that we shall cross the road safely, nor that the aeroplane we catch will deliver us safely to our destination, but we weigh up the risks and the benefits and make the necessary decisions on a daily basis.

> **Lectins:** antibiotic-like proteins produced by, *inter alia*, plants often in response to pests or diseases.

Assessing risks and benefits

We need to address the various concerns commonly expressed by the public and undertake a risk–benefit assessment.

Food safety

In May 2000 a group of ten scientists and physicians calling themselves 'Physicians and Scientists for Responsible Application of Science and Technology' (PSRAST) put out a document entitled *The safety of genetically engineered foods – reasons to expect hazards and the risk of their appearance* (http://www.psrast.org/defknfood.htm). They conclude that there is no doubt that genetic engineering of plants and animals may result in them containing unintended substances that are harmful to consumers. The PSRAST document considers GM foods to be inherently unsafe and calls on governments to withdraw these foods. We shall now consider some of the issues raised in the PSRAST article.

Genetic engineering may introduce unexpected, harmful substances into food

PSRAST claims that, since it is impossible to guide the insertion of a gene into a particular part of the plant's genetic material, this will upset the normal control of DNA over metabolic processes, resulting in unpredictable effects on the plant's metabolism. The scientists also claim that there is no way of knowing what the effect of a foreign protein will be on the metabolism of an organism. Furthermore, genes are context-dependent and may have unpredictable effects in a foreign environment.

It is true that scientists cannot yet guide a gene into a particular region of DNA. However, there is absolutely no evidence that the genetic modification of crop plants has in any way adversely affected plant metabolism. Indeed, developers of GM plants monitor very carefully any potential changes in metabolism. Most of the extensive testing of GM plant products assesses whether there has been any change in the levels of key nutrients and **anti-nutrients** in the plant, and whether this has caused any changes in plant metabolism. Metabolic testing of GM crops is far more rigorous than testing of foods derived from either conventional breeding, in which tens of thousands of genes are randomly combined, or from mutagenesis, in which changes in plant metabolism occur at a reasonably high level.

> **Anti-nutrient:** a substance that counteracts the effect of a nutrient by, for example, making it unavailable to the plant or animal.

Promoter genes may cause unintended problems

The PSRAST article goes on to discredit the use of the promoter that scientists often use to allow the plant to 'read' a foreign gene (see Chapter 2). They claim that these promoters also stimulate the activity of surrounding native genes, with potentially deleterious consequences.

Again they provide no example of such an effect because the statement is incorrect. Scientists insert strong promoters in front of the introduced gene to enable the plant to read it efficiently and produce high levels of protein product. However, the gene also carries a 'termination signal' at the end, so the promoter can only direct the reading of that particular gene. In fact, the promoter the authors refer to is found in plant viruses that naturally infect many of the vegetables we enjoy, so they too contain the promoter DNA.

Genetic engineering introduces new and unknown proteins into food

The authors state that most of the foreign proteins produced by genetic engineering did not previously occur in our food. They therefore claim that, without extensive food safety assessment, there is no way of knowing that it is safe to eat food containing such proteins.

The authors are simply not correct. Typically, proteins introduced into GM plants are from families of proteins with a history of safe use and consumption; for example, the proteins introduced to confer protection against insect pests are the same ones that organic farmers use to protect plants against insects. During the 1960s and 1970s scientists carried out extensive safety tests on this family of proteins, with some tests involving human volunteers. The tests for acute toxicity, sub-chronic and chronic toxicity confirmed that these proteins are safe (FAO/WHO, 2000).

The protein introduced to confer tolerance to the herbicide Roundup comes from a family of proteins present in plants and fungi that we consume. These include maize, soybeans and even the yeast present in beer and yoghurt.

The viral coat proteins used to confer resistance to plant viruses are already present at much higher levels in virally-infected plants than the levels found in GM virus-resistant plants. It is therefore scientifically incorrect to say that these proteins never previously existed in food, or that they are unsafe or untested.

Regulatory genes may cause unpredictable complications

The authors claim that the inserted gene may inadvertently include regulatory genes that could cause unpredictable complications. As I shall discuss in Chapter 8, the regulatory authorities require a detailed characterisation of the introduced DNA. This often includes the complete sequence of the gene and any other pieces of DNA inserted into the plant.

Fusion proteins could cause allergies

The paper refers rather vaguely to so-called fusion proteins and concludes that these could become allergenic (cause allergies). Presumably the authors mean that the DNA inserted into the plant could link to a gene from the parent cell and be expressed as two linked or 'fused' proteins. As discussed above, the genes inserted into plant DNA contain a termination sequence. Unless the inserted gene loses this termination sequence, the inserted DNA will not form a protein fused to one of the plant's own proteins. Again, the requirement for a full molecular characterisation of the GM product addresses this possibility. If termination sequences were to be deleted, the researchers would examine the possibility of a fusion protein. If the plant could indeed produce such a protein, the researchers would conduct a full safety assessment, including detailed allergy and toxicity assessments. In fact, the claim that fusion proteins could cause allergies is not grounded in science. Indeed, a fusion protein is no more likely to cause allergies than any other protein.

Internationally, scientists have agreed to subject every plant biotechnology product to appropriate testing for allergens. These tests are based on sound scientific principles. Scientists test all introduced or expressed proteins in GM crops for their similarity to known allergens. They compare, for instance, their amino acid sequences and key chemical properties, such as stability to heat and to digestive enzymes in the gastrointestinal tract. They also assess the levels of these proteins in food, since the level of consumption of a protein is an important component of an allergy assessment. Based on sound scientific information from these tests, scientists can assess the safety of proteins introduced or expressed by inserted DNA.

Problems with food safety testing

The authors claim that it is not possible to assess with a high degree of accuracy the risk of eating GM foods. They claim that:

- We do not clearly understand the genetic control of cell function: we are therefore unable to predict the outcome of eating GM foods.
- Laboratory experiments with genetic engineering have been very limited. Only short-term studies have been conducted on experimental animals and therefore we cannot predict the effects of slow-acting proteins.
- We have very limited experience of GM foods as they have only been on the market for about five years. Moreover, as GM foods have not been labeled, scientists have been unable to compare the health of people who have and have not been eating these foods.

PSRAST claims that safety testing of GM foods is problematic because genetic engineering may give rise to unexpected and unpredictable substances. The authors then compare the testing of GM foods with the testing of medical drugs.

It is not correct to say that we have a poor understanding of the genetic control of cell function. Although we do not, and probably never shall, understand every single interaction in the cell, by the time we have fully unravelled a given plant's genome, we have an enormous body of knowledge on the subject. In fact, we know a lot more about the biology and biochemistry of the cell and the likely impacts of genes and proteins than we do about the effects of plant breeding or the environment on the final composition of and interactions within the cell. The effects of introducing one or two genes are much easier to study and predict than the way current crop varieties have been developed. Yet, current crop varieties have afforded us the safest food that we have ever enjoyed.

Most animal feeding trials with GM crops are short-term studies, if one defines short-term feeding as the whole lifetime of an animal. For example, many GM products that are appropriate for such testing are fed to chickens from the time they are born to the time they are butchered. Chickens gain weight at an extremely rapid rate, increasing body weight by approximately fifty-fold over their lifetime (FAO/WHO, 2000).

Therefore, this type of study allows scientists to test for both toxic effects and for any, even very minor, effects on the nutrition and wholesomeness of the food or feed. To my knowledge, every product tested in these studies has shown the GM product to be as safe, wholesome and nutritious as the conventional product.

Furthermore, scientists have shown that the newly produced proteins in GM crops have primarily short-term effects, if they have any effect at all. Therefore, short-term studies are typically conducted at very high exposure levels, under conditions where consumption levels are more than 1 000 times higher than normal rates of consumption in food. Therefore these studies are appropriate to address the safety of proteins produced from inserted DNA. Also, scientists test these proteins to ensure that they are rapidly degraded under conditions that mimic human digestion. Most importantly, the proteins being introduced have a history of safe use.

The authors make a scientifically inappropriate comparison between testing food in the same way that pharmaceuticals are tested. Pharmaceuticals are single chemicals whereas foods contain tens of thousands of different components. In the case of pharmaceuticals, scientists can test the single compound at very high levels in animals. This is neither possible nor appropriate with foods. The questions asked are different and therefore the methods used must be different. Scientific experts around the world, including the United Nations Food and Agricultural Organisation and the

World Health Organisation (FAO/WHO, 1996), have assessed this. The world's leading scientists have continued to agree on the appropriate testing for plant biotechnology products (FAO/WHO, 1991, 1996, 2000; WHO 1995; OECD 1993, 1997, 2000).

If, as the authors suggest, we treat GM crops and foods as pharmaceuticals and subject them to double blind tests in human volunteers over decades, then we can say goodbye to GM crops. The costs would be totally prohibitive. Perhaps this is precisely the motivation behind this article: the complete abandonment of the use of GM crops. As I shall point out in Chapter 10, the advantages of the use of GM crops far outweigh the largely hypothetical risks proposed in the PSRAST article.

The development of 'superweeds'

Can a GM crop become a 'superweed', in other words, a weed that is difficult or even impossible to kill and can therefore wreak havoc on the environment? Can a gene coding for a trait such as herbicide resistance pass from a crop to a weedy relative and hence generate a 'superweed'? Let us consider this potential in some actual crops.

Oilseed rape

The concern about 'superweeds' is expressed particularly in the case of oilseed rape (canola) that is resistant to the herbicide glyphosate. Oilseed rape does have some weedy relatives that it can cross-pollinate, so the concern is a valid one. However, to put it into perspective, crops resistant to weedkillers have been bred by conventional means for some 50 years and the spread of resistance was investigated in detail 20 years ago (Holliday and Puwain, 1980). There is absolutely no sign that natural resistance to, for example, the herbicide triazine in canola has spawned 'superweeds'. Gene flow from fields of these plants could carry the resistance gene into weedy relatives. Has this resulted in 'superweeds'? Of course not, and by the same token it is unlikely to occur from GM plants. There is no difference in gene flow from a GM plant or from a classically bred plant.

Many of our domesticated crop plants have been capable of outcrossing with wild plants for centuries. This has not resulted in hybrid weeds as the crosses are rare and the production of fertile hybrids even rarer. As Darwin pointed out in his work on the origin of species in 1859, viable, fertile hybrids that are able to compete successfully in the same environment as either parent species are extremely rare.

Wheat

People have grown wheat in the Middle East for ten thousand years in the presence of the very weeds from which it was domesticated. Breeders have produced many different varieties of wheat and, in a number of cases, they have returned to the original weedy plants in order to obtain genetic traits for particular purposes. Nothing has happened; the weeds haven't become more invasive or more difficult to deal with. Present-day wheat does not survive in fallow fields. It disappears within two years, submerged and overtaken by weeds. We have removed from wheat the capability to act like a weed. The genes we have introduced or amplified are fatal to its weedy qualities.

Poplar trees

When some anti-GMO groups destroyed poplar trees with reduced levels of lignin, the compound that gives trees their strength, their justification was that the introduced genes would contaminate the poplar gene pool forever. It is hard to visualise how a wild poplar tree with a very low lignin content would survive in the wild. Conditions are hard and natural selection is ruthless. Even if there is a low rate of genetic exchange between a GM crop in a field and a weedy relative, the weed will only retain that gene if it gives it an advantage in the struggle to survive.

Bt crops

We have briefly discussed *Bt* crops and whether the acquisition of this gene might increase the plant's weediness because of improved insect resistance. Any self-respecting weed already has the genetic capabilities within its population to deal with any predatory insect; otherwise it will not be a weed for very long!

Introduced plants or alien species are the real 'superweeds'. How many aliens exist in South Africa alone? In the Western Cape, the Port Jackson willow and various species of the genus *Hakea* spring to mind. *Lantana camara*, *Datura* species (trumpet flowers) and various acacias are invasive in other parts of the country. And who has not heard of the dreaded scourge of water hyacinth on many of our fresh water lakes and dams (Richardson *et al.*, 1997)?

Preventing the development of 'superweeds'

If there is a possibility that a GM crop could cross-pollinate a weedy relative and thereby increase its weediness, we can take steps to minimise this. The goal for release into the field for field testing purposes must be minimal opportunity for pollen escape, coupled with rapid identification and eradication of supposed hybrids. This is a simple goal and the following recommendations are generally practised already. Firstly, we must give attention to reported isolation distances for the crop in question:

- There should be no crop relatives within possible pollen exchange distances of the field site. In some cases this will prove difficult, given that some insects commonly travel distances of more than a kilometre.
- Farmers can plant a barrier strip of non-GM plants around the crop to serve as a pollen trap and reduce pollen flow out of the field.
- Application of a post-harvest herbicide or mechanical cultivation of the isolation area around the field could effectively reduce escape.

Secondly, we should study the 'crossability' between the crop and wild relatives that occur in the area of cultivation. More importantly, we must estimate the fitness of any hybrids produced. Data such as these will provide policy makers and field testing agents with necessary information regarding the potential for transgene persistence and the nature and magnitude of ecological risk (Arriola, 1999). It is, of course, ironic that 'terminator' technology, the one technology that could prevent transfer of genes via cross-pollination (see Chapter 3), has been abandoned due to public pressure.

Once a transgenic plant has been released it can never be withdrawn

Another argument against GM crops is that once a transgenic plant has been released it can never be withdrawn. However, as mentioned above, all domesticated crop plants lack the genetic variability and weedy characteristics of wild plants and quickly disappear from fallow fields (Trewavas, 1999).

This argument was raised with considerably greater justification in the mid-1970s when genetic engineering first began. The targets in those days were bacteria being engineered to produce pharmaceuticals and industrially important proteins. In those cases the concern was completely under-standable: once you release bacteria you can never withdraw them as you cannot even see them! But in all the years since 1994 when the first genetic engineering experiments were carried out, no single case of a 'runaway' genetically engineered organism has occurred. Why not? The prime reason is that organisms, particularly small bacteria, containing foreign genes are at a disadvantage due to what is called 'genetic load'. Foreign genes take their toll on the host organism and will only be maintained if they provide an advantage. For instance, antibiotic resistance genes will only be maintained if the organism encounters the particular antibiotic. The same is true of herbi-cide resistance. There is simply no evidence to support the argument that 'runaway' transgenic plants could become herbicide-resistant 'superweeds'.

Vatican experts OK GM plants and animals

One may not agree with everything that comes out of the Vatican, but its proclamations have a major impact. On 12 October 1999 members of the Pontifical Academy for Life presented two volumes of documents on ethics and genetic technology. This represented more than two years of discussion and study. The Vice-President of the Academy stated, 'We are increasingly encouraged that the advantages of genetic engineering of plants and animals are greater than the risks.' He went on to say, 'We give it a prudent "yes". We cannot agree with the position of some groups that say it is against the will of God to meddle with the genetic make-up of plants and animals.'

(St Louis Review, *22 October 1999, on-line version*)

Genetic modification is 'unnatural' and therefore bad

Over the past 50 years plant breeders have been making 'unnatural' combi-nations between many different species of crops using methods such as embryo rescue and cell culture (Baum *et al.*, 1992). Well-known examples include crosses between wheat and rye to produce triticale, which is grown on about a million hectares worldwide. There are also crosses between rice and sorghum, and between agropyron and wheat (Trewavas, 1999). No one

74 --

protests against these crops. Granted, genetic modification allows scientists to take genes from any living organism and introduce them into plants, but the methods of embryo rescue and cell culture are equally 'unnatural'.

Foreign genes will give rise to allergens

The anti-GM lobby appears to have latched onto the idea that foreign genes inserted into plants could cause consumers to have allergic reactions. Even members of the medical fraternity in the United Kingdom have fuelled this misconception. In the British Medical Association's (BMA) report, *The impact of genetic modification on agriculture, food and health* (http://www.bma.org.uk/news), they state that transgenic products may adversely affect people suffering from **allergies** and that soybeans containing genetic material from Brazil nuts cause reactions in individuals allergic to nuts. They do, however, qualify this with the rather ambiguous statement that animal experiments have suggested that allergenicity would not be a problem! Paraphrased in the media, these remarks raised the spectre of GM food causing severe allergic reactions.

In fact, the reference that the BMA used to back up its claims was a paper by Julie Nordlee and her co-workers (1996). The seed company, Pioneer Hi-Bred International, had transferred an albumin gene from Brazil nuts into soybeans, because this would improve the nutritional profile of soy protein. When they realised that the soybeans might cause allergic reactions in consumers allergic to Brazil nuts, they commissioned a study based at the University of Nebraska. Nordlee and her colleagues tested nine people who were allergic to Brazil nuts and found that eight of them were also allergic to the GM soybeans. As a result, the seed company never commercialised these soybeans and nobody ever became ill. In the public's mind, however, a screening test on a well-established **allergen**, carried out specifically to exclude hazards of this nature, became a threat that unforeseen allergens are lurking in GM food products. On the contrary, one of the most valuable potential applications of GM foods is the removal of possible allergens by deleting the relevant genes!

Regulatory authorities are confident that analysis and testing can minimise the risk of biotechnology introducing allergenic proteins. The most important concern is to prevent the transfer of known allergens into

GM crops, as in the case of Brazil nuts above. There are well-established methods of doing this, including:

1. assessing similarities between the protein introduced into a GM crop and a database of all known allergens;
2. evaluating the introduced protein to see whether it possesses features that are common to allergenic proteins; for example, allergens are:
   - rather resistant to heat and are therefore not destroyed in the cooking process;
   - resistant to the acid conditions found in the stomach;
   - generally resistant to digestion under conditions simulating the gastrointestinal system in humans.

Proteins that are readily digested are unlikely to cause food allergies. However, once again, these must be tested on a case-by-case basis. It is also essential to know whether the protein, encoded by the introduced gene in the transgenic plant, will end up in the food product, and if so, how much will be present.

A workshop at the 37th Annual Conference of the Society of Toxicology held in Seattle, Washington in 1998 considered how this should be accomplished (Kimber *et al.*, 1999). The flow diagram shown in Figure 17 is a simplified version of their suggested protocol, based on the work of Metcalfe *et al.* (1996). An important step in the approach is consideration of the source of the candidate gene and whether it derives from a food or pollen known to cause allergies. If it does, the protein must be analysed by an assay called 'radioallergosorbent test' or RAST. These should be followed up by skin prick tests, which test human subjects for allergic reactions. Positive results lead to a hazard evaluation and either the abandonment of the project or, if the benefits are sufficiently great, the use of specific hazard labels.

Allergen: any substance that causes an allergic reaction.

Allergy: a damaging immune response by the body to a substance (allergen) to which the body has become sensitive.

RAST: radioallergosorbent test; a test to determine whether a compound could cause an allergic reaction in humans.

Testing takes a different route if the protein derives from a source that is not associated with food allergy. Here they compare the sequence of amino acids in the protein with the sequence in known allergens, looking for a match of eight or more contiguous amino acids. If the outcome is positive, the RAST and skin prick tests come into play. If such identity is absent, they conclude that the protein is unlikely to be allergenic. However, the protein should also be analysed for stability (a feature of most allergens) and tested for allergenicity using other methods.

Further technical information about testing GM foods for potential allergens is given in Appendix 1 at the end of the book.

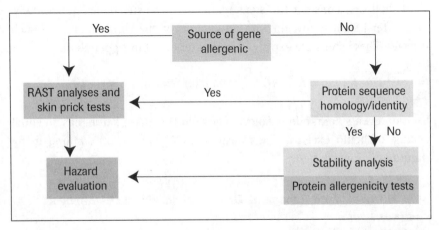

FIGURE 17: Schematic illustration of an approach to the assessment of the allergenic potential of novel food proteins.

More questions and answers

In addition to the risks considered above, the concerned public has many questions about GM crops and foods. I address some of the more frequently asked questions below.

Won't genes be transferred from GM plants to other organisms, causing harmful effects?

Gene transfer from a GM plant to a bacterium, or to humans or animals is called **horizontal gene transfer**. It is the movement of genetic information between sexually unrelated organisms (different species). This is in contrast to **vertical gene transfer** that occurs from parent to offspring. In this section we consider the evidence for such transfer and its possible consequences. You can find more detailed technical information in Appendix II at the end of the book.

Many of the concerns regarding horizontal gene transfer are due to the feeding of transgenic maize or soybean to farm animals such as cows and sheep. The public is also concerned about the transfer of genes giving rise to antibiotic resistance. Can these genes exacerbate the already high levels of antibiotic-resistant bacteria?

I shall first consider the steps required to transfer genes horizontally. Thereafter I shall follow up with an analysis of the consequences of such transfer. These steps are explained in greater detail in Appendix II.

Step 1: The transgenic DNA must be excised from the maize chromosome

Excision events are random, so every gene in the maize kernel has an equal chance of being excised. The transgenic DNA will be one among many thousands of maize genes.

Step 2: The excised transgenic DNA must survive digestion by a ruminant animal like a cow or sheep

Once ingested, DNA released from maize kernels is exposed to digestive enzymes from various animal tissues, including the salivary glands, the pancreas and the intestine. These enzymes cleave most of the DNA into small fragments. The smallest fragment of DNA that could contain a gene coding for antibiotic resistance is about 900 base pairs (a stretch of DNA carrying 900 pairs of bases, A-T or G-C). Most DNA will be rapidly digested into much smaller fragments in a matter of hours.

Step 3: Rumen bacteria must take up the released DNA

Some bacteria can take up DNA from the environment in a process called **transformation**. So far, despite numerous attempts, there have been no reports of the predominant species of rumen bacteria being naturally transformable (Salyers, 1998). However, although this is extremely unlikely, it is not impossible.

DNA uptake is a random event. Therefore a gene coding for antibiotic resistance competes with the rest of the DNA in the plant genome and DNA from other dietary sources for transfer into a bacterium. The maize genome alone contains enough DNA to code for at least a million genes. The chance of an antibiotic resistance gene entering a bacterium in the rumen is vanishingly small.

Having considered the steps required for horizontal gene transfer from transgenic maize to rumen bacteria, let us consider the possible consequences of such a genetic acquisition. If rumen bacteria were to acquire a gene for antibiotic resistance, would this gene be expressed and make the protein that results in antibiotic resistance? So far this hasn't occurred in any rumen bacteria tested (*ibid.*). The bacteria would have to acquire promoters that inform an organism that 'the gene starts here'. We discussed promoters in Chapter 2.

Although the risk of rumen bacteria acquiring and expressing an antibiotic resistance gene from transgenic maize is extremely low, it is not impossible. We must therefore consider the consequences of such acquisition (see Appendix II). However, of greater concern is the general overuse of antibiotics and the consequent increase in antibiotic-resistant bacteria in the environment.

Horizontal gene transfer: transfer of genes between different species that are sexually unrelated.

Vertical gene transfer: the normal method of gene transfer from male and female parents to their offspring.

Ruminant: an animal that chews the cud. Part of its stomach, the rumen, contains bacteria that degrade the fibre in its diet.

Transformation: the ability of some bacteria to take up DNA from their surroundings.

CHAPTER 5: COST-BENEFIT ANALYSIS – IS IT WORTH IT?

Is it safe to eat meat, milk and eggs from livestock and poultry fed on GM crops?

Yes, according to the Federation of Animal Science Societies, comprising over 10 000 animal, dairy and poultry scientists. They have reviewed all the data available worldwide from research studies of which results have been published in refereed, peer-reviewed journal articles. These research results show conclusively that feeding GM crops to livestock and poultry has no effect on the nutritional value or safety of meat, milk or eggs. A number of other studies have shown that the transgenic DNA does not end up in meat, milk or eggs of animals fed grain from GM crops.

Can antibiotic resistance genes be transferred from GM crops to microorganisms in the environment?

Although no one has been able to show that soil bacteria take up genes for antibiotic resistance when exposed to transgenic plant material under natural conditions, Gebhard and Smalla (1998) were able to detect horizontal gene transfer under laboratory conditions. Whether this could occur in nature is highly unlikely but needs to be tested (see Appendix II; Thomson, 2001). Note also that there is widespread resistance to antibiotics and herbicides among soil microbes, both because of selection pressure from naturally occurring antibiotic-producing fungi and bacteria in the soil, and because of repeated applications of herbicides.

While horizontal gene transfer can and does occur, such events are rare and need to be seen in the context of evolutionary time. Although many scientists consider the use of antibiotic resistance genes in transgenic crops to be safe, there is a public perception that this could add to the already high levels of antibiotic resistance in pathogenic bacteria. Scientists and regulators are therefore seeking alternative transformation technologies that do not introduce antibiotic resistance genes into GM crops and foods.

Can we demand zero risks from GM crops and foods?

Scientists have carried out numerous assessments of the safety of GM crops and foods. The National Academy of Sciences in the USA reports that it is not aware of any evidence to suggest that genetically modified foods on the market today are unsafe to eat. Plants engineered genetically through modern molecular techniques pose no greater health or environmental risks than those modified by conventional breeding practices (http://www.nas.edu). The United States Congressional Committee on Science draws similar conclusions in the article 'Seeds of Opportunity' (http://www.house.gov/science), as do the Royal Society of the United Kingdom (http://www.royalsoc.ac.za), the Nuffield Foundation (http://www.nuffield.org;), the European Molecular Biology Organisation (http://www.embo.org;) and the Royal Society of South Africa (http://www.uct.ac.za/org/RSSA).

There is a great deal of loose talk and many unsubstantiated claims about the danger of GM crops and the foods derived from them. The Organisation for Economic Cooperation and Development (OECD) convened a meeting in Edinburgh, Scotland in February 2000 to consider these very safety issues. The OECD is an organisation of industrialised countries epitomised by the G8 nations: the 'haves' as opposed to the 'have nots'. Of the 400 participants invited, about equal numbers were for, against and undecided regarding GM technology. During the final session, the Chair was trying to determine what the participants agreed upon, where they disagreed and about what they could not make decisions because of a lack of data. A speaker raised the issue of the dangers of GM technology. The Chair, most forcefully, stopped the speaker in her tracks and appealed to the audience to come forward immediately with any information regarding this lack of safety. The only example that anyone could give was a case of tryptophan impurities in Japan. As was explained, however, this had nothing to do with GM technology. However, as the safety of GM-derived foods is such an emotive subject, the next chapter is devoted to this topic.

On the question of zero risk, we do not demand zero health or environmental risks from any other technology or service, including medical treatment, providing water and power to cities or building affordable housing. In all these cases, legislation and policing minimise risks to maintain acceptable safety standards. In the case of GMO technology the analysis needs to include the risks associated with the practices that GM crops help to curtail. For example, what are the risks of using insecticides? What do we gain by planting crops that do not need insecticides? Next evaluate whether the GM crop poses a risk that is known or unknown, probable or implausible. If you can improve the nutrient content of rice, resulting in less disease or blindness, what risks are you willing to accept? Too often, when dealing with issues around genetic modification, we forget

CHAPTER 5: COST-BENEFIT ANALYSIS – IS IT WORTH IT?

to look at the dangers we are reducing by using this new technology. Is there zero risk associated with conventional plant breeding? In this case we cross two or more organisms and mix tens of thousands of genes, the functions of most of which are unknown. We can assess the risks and benefits of this experiment, carried out over the last 10 000 years or so. There have been some unwanted traits; for instance many people are allergic to wheat. Overall, however, it has been vastly successful. Genetic engineering is as safe or safer than conventional breeding. It is unequivocally more precise.

Will poor farmers in developing countries become dependent on commercial biotechnology companies?

Poor farmers in developing countries should become no more reliant on biotechnology companies than they are on pharmaceutical companies or companies providing capital equipment for infrastructure. Yet no one suggests banning these commodities. GM technology may help to improve the lot of poor farmers. In a commercial relationship, corporations are as dependent on their customers as their customers are on them. If a technology is banned, no one benefits from it. There is no obligation on poor farmers to purchase GM seed, nor is traditional seed unavailable to farmers who save their seed to plant the next season. Whether from the developed or developing world, farmers will buy GM seed at a premium compared to the cost of traditional seed only if it results in improved crop yields.

One of the key concerns of farmers in developing countries is trying to reduce yield swings between good and bad years. GM crops can help overcome this feast or famine effect. GM crops are only one tool in the struggle for sustainable agriculture in developing countries, but they are critical tools because of their ease of use and their dramatic yield increases, especially when arable land is scarce. On the whole, the net increase in yield and crop protection outweigh the increased cost of the seeds. If this were not the case, GM seed producers would be unable to sell their stock.

Having said this, governments, international aid agencies and industry should provide training, access to technology and experience to enable developing countries to develop GM seed which is designed to meet their particular needs. Internationally, we need to refocus agricultural aid away from 'crisis management' during a famine or a flood and towards sustainable agriculture that will avoid famine. GM seeds are part of this approach.

Will GM crops accelerate the trend towards fewer crop varieties? Will this make agriculture more vulnerable?

The reverse is more likely to be true. Conventional breeding melds a particular trait of interest with other desirable traits. This entails the breeding out of unwanted traits over many generations. Genetic engineering allows us to add a single desired trait to an already optimised breed of plant rapidly and directly. This will in fact make it easier to diversify crops; for example, the Roundup Ready trait has been introduced into more than 1 000 different soybean varieties.

In addition, as I pointed out in Chapter 4, the development of insect-resistant crops is resulting in a decrease in the use of chemical insecticides. As a result, insects not seen for years on farms are returning. Consequently insect-eating birds are returning. In parts of South Africa, they have even been found nesting in cotton fields. The use of GM crops is resulting in an increase in biodiversity.

Is genetic engineering the only way to increase food production?

No, there are numerous ways of increasing food production. Genetic engineering is just another tool. It is important not to allow the food-rich first world countries to dictate to the developing world in this regard. Biotechnology is a very inexpensive way to increase yields and to reduce damage due to pests and disease. It requires no training or knowledge on the part of a farmer and the technology is built into the seed, which all farmers know how to use. It is also an inexpensive way to decrease the use of environmentally harmful chemicals, although that is hardly a criterion for its use in the developing world. Third world farmers are the quintessential organic farmers: they have seldom or never been able to afford to use chemicals. Other ways of increasing food production include improvements in agricultural practices. Although these alternatives can be quite complex, they should not be abandoned. GM crops are only part of the answer. Many other practices are equally important.

Can genetic engineering deal with widespread malnutrition?

There are no easy answers to the problem of malnutrition. One of the key issues is the cost and difficulty of transporting agricultural products to areas in need. GM seeds are only part of the solution. They can contain valuable nutrients not found in traditional seeds. They can be designed to grow in harsher soils and climates, and to withstand diseases and pests. However, dealing with widespread malnutrition will also require improved transportation, the end of wars and corruption, a decrease in the rate of population expansion, and a whole host of other socio-economic interventions.

If supermarkets are withdrawing GM foods from their shelves, surely they must be bad?

We need some perspective here. Supermarkets acknowledge that there is nothing wrong with GM foods, yet they withdraw these foods from their shelves and say that all of their own brand products are GM-free. If the public will not buy GM foods, supermarkets will not sell them. The consumer is king. By rejecting GM foods, supermarkets and food processors are denying their customers access to foods that may in the future bring them health benefits and improved flavour. Ironically, the fact that supermarkets continue to promote and sell tobacco, alcohol, fatty foods and sweets is of little concern to the public. GM foods are bad but fast foods are fine. If consumers are looking for healthy foods, then they should be aware that food retailers are flying a shaky flag, nutritionally speaking.

If we were to rank some general risks, smoking and alcohol would be at the top, sun tanning and traffic accidents a little lower down, industrial pollution and naturally occurring toxins in food somewhat further down. GM food would be at the bottom of the list.

Isn't GM a conspiracy by a few multinational companies to control world food production and make enormous profits?

It is a fallacy that only multinationals are involved in the development of improved crops through genetic modification. There are over 1 000 smaller listed and unlisted companies involved in these developments. In addition universities and research institutes, funded by governments, aid agencies (notably the Rockefeller Foundation) and the institutions themselves, spend millions of dollars each year on these initiatives. Indeed, on 9 May 2000 a US Senate spending committee approved $30 million in new funding for biotechnology research projects to help developing countries. However, it is also ridiculous to criticise companies for wanting to make profits. After all, that is why they are in business and what their shareholders expect of them.

Shouldn't these companies bear total liability for any harm to the environment and public health?

Responsibilities should be the same as they have always been. Inventors should be liable for the safe operation of their products; for example, biotechnologists should continue to check for and advertise allergens and environmental impacts. Growers should be responsible for following guidelines to safeguard the environment. Processors should be responsible for safe, hygienic handling of materials; and consumers should be responsible for knowing their own health concerns and consuming prudently, as well as minding the expiry dates on their purchases. Each party shares in the responsibility. No one party has 'total' responsibility.

In summary ...

Hopefully the information supplied in this chapter will help you to decide that indeed it is worth it, as long as regulations are in place and we evaluate each GM crop on a case-by-case basis.

The trade-offs between benefits and risks vary in different regions and between different economies. Regionally the balance may vary for different segments of the population.

In judging new technologies we should bear in mind that the potential of present-day agriculture to meet future demands is under strain. The area of available arable land is decreasing with urban development, and the growth in productivity is levelling off. GM technologies, if developed under appropriate conditions, offer the potential to provide solutions that can be part of a range of answers to the problem of providing the whole world with sufficient food of the necessary nutritional quality.

References and further reading

Arriola, P. E. (1999) Risks of escape and spread of engineered genes from transgenic crops to wild relatives. AgBiotechNet.
(http:/agbio.cabweb.org/REVIEWS/misc/arriola.htm)
Baum M., Lagudah, E. S. and Appels, R. (1992) Wide crosses in cereals. *Annual Review of Plant Physiology and Plant Molecular Biology.* Vol. 43, pp. 117–143.

FAO/WHO. (1991) Strategies for assessing the safety of foods produced by biotechnology. *Report of a Joint FAO/WHO Consultation*. WHO, Geneva.

FAO/WHO. (1996) Biotechnology and food safety. Report of a Joint JAO/WHO Consultation. FAO, Food and Nutrition Paper 61.

FAO/WHO. (2000) Safety aspects of genetically modified foods of plant origin. WHO, Geneva. Report of a Joint FAO/WHO Expert Consultation on foods derived from biotechnology, 29 May – 2 June 2000.

Gebhard, F. and Smalla, K. (1998) Transformation of *Acinetobacter* sp. strain BD413 by transgenic sugar beet DNA. *Applied and Environmental Microbiology*. Vol. 64, pp. 1550–1554.

Holliday, R. J. and Puwain, P. D. (1980) Evolution of herbicide resistance in *Senecio vulgaris:* variation in susceptibility to simazine between and within populations *Journal of Applied Ecology*. Vol. 17, pp. 779–791.

Kimber, I., Kerkvliet, N. I. Taylor, S. L. Astwood, J. D. Sarlo, K. and Dearman, R. J. (1999) Toxicology of protein allergenicity: prediction and characterisation. *Toxicological Sciences*. Vol. 48, pp. 157–162.

Metcalfe, D. D., Astwood, J. D., Townsend, R., Sampson, H. A., Taylor, S. L. and Fuchs, R. L. (1996) Assessment of the allergenic potential of foods derived from genetically engineered crop plants. *Critical Reviews in Food Science and Nutrition*. Vol. 36, pp. S165–S186.

Nordlee, J. A., Taylor, S. L, Townsend, J. A., Thomas, L. A. and Bush, R. K. (1996) Identification of a Brazil-nut allergen in transgenic soybeans. *New England Journal of Medicine*. Vol. 334, pp. 688–692.

OECD (Organisation for Economic Cooperation and Development). (1993) *Safety evaluation of foods produced by modem biotechnology: concepts and principles*. OECD, Paris.

OECD. (1997) OECD Documents. *Report of the OECD Workshop on the toxicological and nutritional testing of novel foods*. OECD, Paris.

Richardson, D. M., MacDonald, I. A. W., Hoffmann, J. H. and Henderson, L. (1997) Alien plant invasions. In: Cowling, R. M, Richardson, D. M. and Pierce, S. M. (eds) *Vegetation of Southern Africa*. Cambridge University Press, Cambridge, UK.

Salyers, A. (1998) Genetically engineered foods: safety issues associated with anti-biotic resistance genes. (http//www.healthsci.tufts.edu/apua/salyersreport.htm)

Thomson, J. A. (2001) Horizontal transfer of DNA from GM crops to bacteria and to mammalian cells. *Journal of Food Science*. Vol. 66, pp. 188-193.

Trewavas, A. (1999) Much food, many problems. *Nature*. Vol. 402, pp. 231–232.

WHO. (1995) Application of the principles of substantial equivalence to the safety evaluation of foods and food components from plants derived by modern biotechnology. Report of a WHO Workshop. World Health Organisation, Geneva.

Chapter 6

GM crops and food safety

Evaluating the safety of GM foods

Regulatory agencies in many countries including Europe, North America, Japan, Australia, Canada and South Africa require all GM crops to be subjected to extensive safety trials and field trial evaluations before being released. Such procedures can take from seven to ten years before final commercialisation of a new GM crop (Beever and Kemp, 2000).

All agencies call for extensive characterisation and safety evaluation of the novel protein resulting from the inserted gene, including:

- measuring protein accumulation levels in various parts of the plant;
- testing plants for growth and development characteristics to ensure that the inserted DNA does not disrupt any genes critical for normal plant development or alter the expression of important genes;
- extensive compositional analyses to ensure that no unintended but nutritionally significant changes have occurred in the plant;
- determining the stability of the gene(s) and their inheritance patterns.

For ease of reference, a list of documents is provided dealing with international food safety issues in Appendix III at the end of this book.

Protein safety

Assessing the safety of a protein starts even before a gene is introduced into a plant. Scientists select proteins that are well characterised and plants that have a history of safe use. The more we know before embarking on the formal safety assessment, the more sure we can be that the vigorous testing procedures will confirm that the protein is safe.

The first step in the food safety assessment is to purify the protein and determine its molecular weight, solubility and stability. The next stage involves acute toxicity studies feeding the protein to mice at doses hundreds to thousands of times higher than humans would receive when consuming the GM crop. The testers monitor changes in animal weight and make clinical observations over a period of at least 14 days. At the end of the test period they kill the animals and examine the major organs. Any adverse finding, including poor weight gain, abnormal appearance of tissues or organs or, of course, any toxicity leads to more testing or possible abandonment of the specific plant line.

An important consideration is whether the animals or humans who might consume the novel protein could have had previous exposure to it. For instance, the gene for herbicide tolerance in GM soybeans and maize codes for a protein similar to one that occurs naturally in all plants and bacteria, including maize. Ever since animals and people first started to eat plants, they have consumed this protein safely. Equally, organic farmers have used insecticidal *Bt* proteins for the last 40 years without problems.

Having said that, companies have carried out animal feeding trials and *in vitro* studies on both herbicide-tolerant and insect-resistant crops using simulated gastric and intestinal fluids. The protein that confers herbicide tolerance was found to degrade readily in simulated gastric and intestinal fluids, suggesting that it will also break down in the mammalian digestive tract upon ingestion as a component of food or feed. There were no deleterious effects due to the administration of the protein to mice by **gavage** at doses more than 1 000 times the anticipated consumption level of food products potentially containing the protein (Harrison *et al.*, 1996).

Companies have also subjected the *Bt* protein that confers insect protection in maize to a simulated digestion study. In gastric fluid, more than 90% of the protein degraded within 30 seconds of incubation. To put this rapid degradation into perspective, approximately 50% of solid food empties from the human stomach within two hours, whereas liquid empties in approximately 25 minutes. The *Bt* protein is relatively resistant to further digestion by enzymes found in the intestine. As expected, the *Bt* protein did not degrade substantially after being incubated in intestinal fluid for 19.5 hours. Therefore most of the degradation will occur in the stomach. A mouse study performed using the *Bt* protein had no adverse effects

(Sanders *et al.*, 1998). There have been similar results from gavage studies performed on other *Bt* proteins such as that found in potatoes resistant to the Colorado potato beetle (Lavrik *et al.*, 1996) and the *Bt* protein present in cotton resistant to bollworms and budworms (Betz *et al.*, 2000).

Gavage: the artificial administration of food by, for example, feeding via tubes.

In vitro: in a test tube (Latin *vitrum* = glass).

Whole food testing

The testing of whole, complex foods is not as clear-cut as the testing of purified proteins. For instance, feeding animals exclusively on *Bt* maize would lead to nutritional imbalances. Such imbalances may result in adverse effects completely unrelated to the specific properties of *Bt* maize. Due to the bulk of such foods and their effect on an animal's appetite we can usually only feed experimental animals at low multiples of the amounts that might be present in the human diet. Identifying potential adverse effects and relating these conclusively to an individual characteristic of the food can be extremely difficult.

In practice, very few foods consumed today have been subjected to any toxicological studies, yet we generally accept that they are safe to eat. In South Africa we have the example of the peppadew, a member of the Capsicum family to which peppers and chillies also belong. It was found in the Eastern Cape province, and was commercialised in the early 1990s. The developers carried out no food safety or toxicity tests, yet it has proven to be very popular. Indeed, there is no such thing as a safe food; there is only the safe use of food. Studies to determine food safety have to be custom designed on a case-by-case basis and generally use a combination of *in vivo* and *in vitro* techniques.

Assessing the safety of genetically modified foods or, more correctly, foods derived from genetically modified crops, is a stepwise process aided by a series of structured questions.

Safety of GM foods

Factors taken into account when assessing the safety of GM foods include:

■ identity;
■ source;
■ composition;
■ effects of processing and cooking;
■ the transformation process;
■ the recombinant DNA (e.g. stability of inserted genes, potential for gene transfer);
■ the protein produced by the introduced DNA, including function, mode of action, potential toxicity and potential allergenicity;
■ possible secondary effects from gene expression or the disruption of host DNA or metabolic pathways (including composition of macro-, micro- and anti-nutrients, endogenous toxicants, allergens, and physiologically active substances);
■ potential intake and dietary impact of the genetically modified food.

Scientists generally consider that a rodent sub-chronic study of 90 days duration is the minimum requirement to demonstrate the safety and substantial equivalence to non-GM comparative foods (see page 93) of long-term consumption of novel GM food in the diet. They may need to carry out a short pilot study to ensure that the diet is palatable to the test animals and that levels of incorporation of the test food are appropriate. For instance, it is important that the control diet containing the 'comparator' (the food to which the GM food is being compared) will not produce effects due to the presence of a toxic compound found naturally in traditional foods. The highest dose level used in any animal studies should be the maximal achievable without causing nutritional imbalance. The lowest level should be comparable to the anticipated human intake.

We know very little about the potential long-term effects of any foods, whether conventional or GM foods. Wide genetic variability in the human population confounds such effects, as some individuals may have a greater or lesser predisposition to food-related effects.

Unintended effects

It is theoretically possible that during the course of introducing a specific intended trait into a plant, unintended changes could occur. Scientists accept that the likelihood of such changes is no more than in the case of conventional breeding or mutagenesis; indeed biotechnology is probably less likely to cause unintended changes. The assessment of GM foods therefore involves methods to assess for such unintended effects and evaluate their biological relevance and their impact on food safety.

Factors such as the random insertion of a gene into the plant's DNA can cause these unintended effects. This might disrupt existing genes, modify the expression of proteins or cause new compounds to be formed. Such unintended effects are not specific to GM foods; they are a feature of conventional plant breeding as well. To cope with this problem in both GM technology and plant breeding, we select and discard plants with unusual and undesired characteristics at an early stage. Another procedure used to eliminate unintended effects is consecutive back-crossing, described in Chapter 1. The unintended effects of genetic modification include both:

■ unpredictable effects, and
■ predictable effects, based on **metabolic** connections to the intended effect.

As genetic engineering becomes increasingly precise compared with conventional plant breeding, it is easier to identify the potential unintended effects on metabolic pathways of introducing a novel gene into a crop plant.

Scientists analyse extensively the composition of GM crops. They grow these crops under various conditions and assay for key nutrients and anti-nutrients to ascertain whether unintended changes have occurred. They typically analyse 50–100 different plant components and test a number of varieties of the crop and the parent plants to establish the natural variability of each component. If scientists observe significant unintended changes in a GM plant, they should investigate the biological significance in order to evaluate safety implications. If the differences exceed the natural variations in traditional foods, further assessment is required.

A typical example of unintended differences being incorrectly ascribed to an introduced gene is the case of isoflavones in soybeans. There were claims that Roundup Ready™ soybeans had reduced levels of beneficial nutritional compounds called isoflavones. The American Soybean Association (ASA) refuted this in a statement issued on 23 June 1999 (http://www.oilseeds.org/asa/documents/isobkgndr.htm). Isoflavone components in soybeans are highly variable and environmental factors greatly influence their concentrations. The ASA was confident that the variability noted in GM crops was within the limits of natural variability.

Currently we detect unintended effects by analysing specific compounds. This targeted approach is based on a scientific understanding of the metabolic pathways that could be affected. In order to increase the probability of detecting unintended effects, scientists are developing new methods to identify such changes. This non-targeted approach is still in its infancy. Techniques include the study of whole genomes and the proteins they produce, as well as **micro-arrays**. Techniques that profile the genetic composition of the whole plant may contribute more extensively to the detection of differences than targeted chemical analysis. However, once we identify differences, we will still need to consider their biological and safety implications.

One example of detecting unintended effects by analysing specific compounds comes from the development of transgenic rice low in glutelin for the production of sake. Glutelin is a major storage protein of rice but its presence adversely affects the quality of sake. Scientists found that low-glutelin rice, produced by genetic modification, had unintended high levels of prolamines, a group of proteins rich in the amino acid proline. However, based on their knowledge of glutelin and prolamines, they had predicted this and consequently tested for it (Yoshizawa and Kishi, 1985). In any case, prolamines have no harmful effects.

Another example is the unintended production of carotenoid compounds called xanthophylls in transgenic 'golden rice'. We discussed golden rice, produced to supply vitamin A to people living in Asia (Ye et al., 2000), in Chapter 4. The developers did not expect the plants to produce xanthophylls. However, these compounds are antioxidants and have a positive effect. They help to prevent diseases caused by the conversion of oxygen into toxic free radicals.

Micro-array: a technique used to analyse simultaneously the amount of mRNA produced by different genes present in a sample such as a food product.

Metabolism: all the chemical reactions and physiological changes that occur in living organisms.

Substantial equivalence

Some regulatory authorities use the concept of 'substantial equivalence', developed as a practical approach to assessing the safety of GM foods. The application of the concept is not a safety assessment in itself and does not set out to characterise hazard. Rather, it is used to structure the safety assessment of a GM food relative to a conventional counterpart.

As a starting point, the authorities compare the GM plant and/or foods derived from it with their closest traditional counterpart in order to identify the intended and unintended differences that then become the focus of the safety assessment. This comparative approach takes into account agronomic, genetic and chemical aspects. Only when they have considered all of these aspects can they make an objective assessment of safety. The type and extent of further studies depend on the nature of the differences and whether or not they are well characterised.

Scientists test plant tissues from GM crops for most major nutrients, including total protein and lipids. They also assess possible anti-nutritional factors and specific attributes of a given crop. They feed GM crop materials to sensitive animal species such as chickens, trout, catfish, goats and most farm animal species, and test proteins conferring insect resistance to establish whether they are toxic to non-target organisms including lady-birds, bees and nematodes. They compare the data with those from non-GM varieties of the same crop to determine whether the GM varieties are 'substantially equivalent'.

International scientific experts, including representatives of FAO/WHO and OECD, state that the process by which genes are transferred does not make a living organism harmful. Transferring genes between unrelated species is possible because living organisms are genetically similar. Many genetic traits have been conserved throughout time in microbes, plants and animals. Although an organism may contain a few unique proteins, many plant and animal proteins have similar or closely related functions. For example, both the human brain and rice plants carry the same gene for the production of an enzyme called lysozyme. Furthermore, the transfer of one or a few genes between unrelated species will not turn them into each other.

In contrast, many critics of GM technology do not favour the concept of substantial equivalence. They believe that, because of the nature of the technology involved in the development of a transgenic crop, it cannot possibly be substantially equivalent. Other critics of the concept seem to think that substantial equivalence refers to the end point of a safety assessment, whereas, as explained above, it is merely the starting point. Substantial equivalence is a concept used to identify similarities and differences between the GM food and a comparator with a history of safe food use; this in turn guides the safety assessment process. Figure 18 outlines the process involved in assessing food safety based on substantial equivalence.

FIGURE 18:
A sequential approach to assessing food safety, based on substantial equivalence.

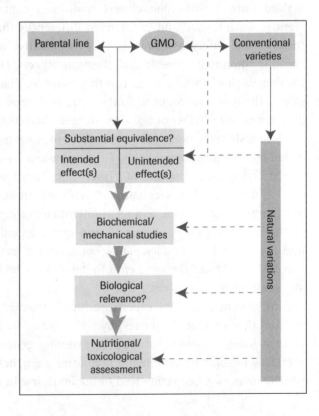

Substantial equivalence of herbicide-resistant soybeans

To test the safety of herbicide-resistant soybeans, scientists fed diets containing processed or ground soybeans to four different animal species: laboratory rats, broiler chickens, catfish and dairy cattle. They compared unmodified parent soybeans with two genetically modified lines. Because many dairy cattle eat raw, unprocessed soybeans, they fed these to lactating dairy cattle. They fed the catfish and broiler chickens processed soybean meal, which is a normal component of their commercial diets. They carried out these studies for four weeks on rats and dairy cows, six weeks on chickens and ten weeks on catfish. Studies done on herbicide-resistant soybeans compared:

- growth;
- feed conversion in rats, catfish and chickens;
- fillet composition in catfish;
- breast muscle and fat pad weights in chickens;
- milk production, milk composition, rumen fermentation and nitrogen digestibility in dairy cows.

In all studies, measured variables were similar for animals fed both GM lines and the parental line (Hammond *et al.*, 1996). This indicated that the feed value of all the soybeans tested is comparable. The results confirmed trials carried out using the purified protein that confers herbicide resistance on soybean (Harrison *et al.*, 1996).

Substantial equivalence of *Bt* crops

In the case of insect-resistance crops, scientists fed potatoes expressing the *Bt* protein and parental non-GM potatoes to rats in a 28-day study. The rats consumed an average of 80 grams of potato per kilogram of body weight per day, which is equivalent to a human consuming 35 to 40 potatoes per day. They observed no differences in food consumption, growth rate, behaviour or gross pathology during these studies (Lavrik *et al.*, 1996). In another study, five male and five female human volunteers ate or inhaled a microbial formulation of *Bt* containing four different *Bt* proteins. The formulation contained live *Bacillus thuringiensis* bacteria. The volunteers received a dose of 1 gram per day for three consecutive days. Scientists monitored stool samples for the presence of the *Bt* organisms. Although stool samples from half of the volunteers contained the *Bt* organisms for at least 30 days after ingestion, the scientists observed no adverse effects in the test subjects. So, in addition to the dosage over three days the volunteers were exposed to *Bt* proteins for at least 30 days without suffering any harmful effects (McClintock *et al.*, 1995).

Consumption of DNA

Animals and humans consume significant quantities of DNA from a wide variety of sources on a daily basis. These include plants, animals, bacteria, fungi and viruses. The relative proportions of DNA in food vary, but may be less than 0.02% and as little as 0.005% (Watson and Thompson, 1988). In humans, dietary intake of DNA can vary widely but is typically in the range of 0.1 to 1 grams per day (Doerfler and Schubbert, 1997). Enzymes in the alimentary tract degrade most of the DNA, making it non-functional. Beever and Kemp (2000) estimate that a dairy cow fed GM maize as forage, maize silage or maize grain will consume GM DNA at a ratio of 1:234 000 to other DNA. This is equivalent to 0.00042% of total dietary DNA. On this basis it appears that exposure to transgenic DNA will be negligible compared with exposure to normal, non-GM crop DNA. Furthermore, upon consumption, the DNA is rapidly degraded.

Who ensures that GM crops pose no threat?

Regulatory authorities consider each GM crop on a case-by-case basis as each has specific potential impacts on the environment. Thus, for example, we must consider the ability of a herbicide-resistant plant to cross-pollinate a potentially weedy relative if such relatives exist in the pollination range of the GM crop. In the case of insect resistance, we need to determine the effect of the protein produced by the introduced gene on non-target insects. Scientists have undertaken a number of studies to determine this. In one such study, Sanders *et al.* (1998) found no significantly harmful effects on honeybees, ladybirds or earthworms. A recent review by Betz *et al.* (2000) summarises data on a variety of *Bt* proteins that have been introduced into GM crops. None of these *Bt* proteins showed negative effects on non-target insects.

We must consider the very real possibility of the development of insects resistant to the *Bt* protein. Three years before the commercialisation of *Bt* maize in the USA the Environmental Protection Agency (EPA) formed a Pesticide Resistance Management Working Group to analyse different resistance-management systems. They favour a dual system in which *Bt* crops produce the toxin in doses high enough to kill essentially 100% of the pests and farmers plan refuges of the corresponding non-*Bt* crop. These refuges will effectively dilute existing resistance genes within the pest population. Refuges do not put a selective pressure on the development of resistance to the *Bt* protein. Rather, pairing between *Bt*-resistant and susceptible pests from refuges should result in less resistant offspring and therefore to an overall delay in the development of resistance.

In order to implement this policy effectively, we must know what percentage of the crop should constitute non-*Bt* refuges. The recommended percentage varies with the crop and geographical location from as low as 5% unsprayed cotton to as high as 50%. In field and greenhouse trials carried out to test these recommendations, Shelton *et al.* (2000) found the following:

■ In greenhouses with no refuges the number of resistance genes in the insect population increased significantly. With 20% refuges this was significantly inhibited.

■ In greenhouses the refuge strategy worked best if the conventional plants were grown separately from the *Bt* plants.

■ In open field trials, treatment of the refuge area with an insecticide reduced the distribution of larvae and led to a relative increase in the resistance gene among insects in the field.

The results do not allow us to predict the time frame for resistance development by specific combinations of *Bt* crops and pests. For each combination we must develop an individual resistance management scheme that considers the biology of the pest, the dosage and type of *Bt* expression in the crop, and specific ecological considerations relating to the geographical location. The refuge strategy recommended by the EPA is a good tool to hinder the development of resistance in target insect pests.

Although most scientists believe that risks to the environment and to animal and human health are largely hypothetical and that current safeguards are adequate, we need to continue with research, especially on long-term effects. Unfortunately, there is no way of 'fast-tracking' such research; long-term effects can only be determined in the long term.

On the other hand

Organic farming and GM crops

Organic farming has a valuable role to play in agriculture. It has a niche market that it serves admirably. However, it is puzzling that organic farmers ban the use of GM technology in their crops. What could be more 'organic' than a gene and the protein it produces? Furthermore, one of the aims of GM technology is to reduce the use of the very chemical herbicides and pesticides that organic farmers want to avoid. It is therefore strange that organically grown crops are viewed as 'good' and 'natural' while GM crops are viewed as 'bad' and 'unnatural'.

In May 2000 the supermarket giant Tesco in the United Kingdom withdrew all its organically grown mushrooms after routine tests showed the possible presence of the deadly *Escherichia coli* bacterium strain O157:H7. Most strains of *E. coli* are harmless but this one can cause serious diarrhoea and even death. In a research paper published a few months earlier in March 2000 (Dingman, 2000), scientists had found that organically produced apple juice and cider had high levels of the same strain of bacterium. The source of these contaminants could be the animal manure that organic farmers use as fertilisers.

Organic farming in countries such as South Africa will probably feed about 2% of the population, and only those who can afford these more expensive products. It has almost no impact on the majority of malnourished people here and in the rest of sub-Saharan Africa. Because organic farmers do not use chemical pesticides, when pests or diseases attack their crops the plants strike back by producing toxins to protect themselves. These compounds, such as proteins called lectins, can also be toxic to animals and humans. People eating organically grown food should be aware of this fact.

Plants produce 'natural' toxins

Plants have been evolving and refining their chemical weapons for at least 500 million years. If these compounds were not effective in deterring predators, the plants producing them would not have been naturally selected. Humans, on the other hand, have not had time to evolve into 'toxic harmony' with all of the plants in their diet. Indeed, very few of the plants that we eat today would have been present in the diet of an African hunter-gatherer. We eat a wide variety of plants that our ancestors did not, such as coffee, cocoa, tea, potatoes, tomatoes, maize, avocados, mangoes, kiwi fruit and, in South Africa, peppadews. In ancient times people used cruciferous vegetables such as cabbage, broccoli, kale, cauliflower and mustard primarily for medicinal purposes. They spread as foods across Europe only in the Middle Ages (Fenwick et al., 1983; McDanell et al., 1988). Natural selection works far too slowly for humans to have evolved specific resistance to the food toxins in these newly introduced plants. Thus we should be aware that when we eat food derived from a plant that has been attacked by bacteria, viruses or insects, we will also consume a variety of toxins that the plant produces to defend itself.

We often assume that, because plants are part of human evolutionary history, whereas synthetic chemicals are recent, the mechanisms that animals have evolved to cope with natural toxic chemicals will fail to protect us against synthetic chemicals. In 1962 Rachel Carson caused a stir with her book *Silent Spring*. She warned that, for the first time in history, every human being was coming into contact with dangerous chemicals, from the moment of conception until death. The world-renowned scientist, Bruce Ames, who developed the 'Ames test' for the rapid detection of mutagenic and potentially carcinogenic compounds, takes issue with this (Ames et al., 1990). Animals and humans have evolved defences that are mostly of a general type, since the number of natural chemicals that might have toxic effects is very large. General defences offer protection not only against natural toxins but also against synthetic chemicals, so animals and humans are well buffered against toxins. Mechanisms include the continuous shedding of cells exposed to toxins, such as the surface layers of the mouth, gastrointestinal tract, skin and lungs, and the induction of a wide variety of general detoxifying mechanisms.

CHAPTER 6: GM CROPS AND FOOD SAFETY

Many natural toxins, some of which have been present throughout vertebrate history, cause cancer in animals and humans; for example, fumonisins produced by fungi or moulds. Insect damage of crops such as maize makes them more susceptible to post-harvest infection by fungi. One of the advantages of insect-resistant GM maize is the decrease in this post-harvest infection and therefore a decrease in the incidence of hazardous fumonisins (see Chapter 3).

Natural toxins can have the same mechanisms of toxicity as synthetic toxins. One example is dioxin. Cabbage and broccoli contain a chemical whose breakdown products act in just the same way as does dioxin, one of the most feared industrial contaminants. Thus it is important to understand that many plants can produce compounds that can be harmful to humans and animals.

Fumonisins: highly toxic compounds produced by fungi or moulds; they can cause cancer.

Greenpeace and GM crops

The opposition of Greenpeace to the use of GM crops is intimately associated with the organic farming movement, which contributes over $100 million to their annual budget. Many scientists who firmly supported Greenpeace in its early days are becoming more and more disillusioned by their abandonment of science and logic. Indeed, Patrick Moore, an ecologist who helped found Greenpeace in the early 1970s, recently quit the organisation for these very reasons. He went so far as to state that pagan beliefs and junk science are influencing the movement's public policy (visit Moore's website http://www.greenspirit.com). William Plaxton, Professor of Biology and Biochemistry at Queen's University in Ontario, Canada, was a former scientific advisor to Greenpeace. He resigned on 9 November 1999, citing fear-mongering and non-scientific attacks on the production and use of GM plants as some of his reasons for leaving.

An example of the illogical behaviour of Greenpeace is that they demand more field testing of GM crops, yet they participate in the destruction of these very field trails. For instance, in July 1999 Greenpeace supporters flattened an experimental crop of Aventis GM maize planted by a Norfolk farmer in the United Kingdom. In the consequent court action the jury voted to acquit all the 'Greenpeace 28' defendants of charges of criminal damage. The British press considered the verdict 'legalised sabotage'. Even Lord Melchet of Greenpeace agreed with farmers' representatives who said that the extraordinary decision gave the green light to wanton vandalism and trespass.

Concerns of organic farmers

One of the concerns of organic farmers, also expressed by Greenpeace, is seed segregation. Organic farmers do not allow their products to contain any genes modified by biotechnological methods. They therefore do not want GM seed mixed with GM-free seed and want farmers to certify that the seed they produce is GM-free. Seed must be segregated in order for organic farmers to be sure that they are buying GM-free seeds. Seed can certainly be segregated but at what additional cost? No feasible segregation systems will deliver 100% GM-free seed. This is impossible. I will return to this issue in Chapter 10.

Organic farmers also want protection from cross-pollination of their crops by GM plants in neighbouring fields. However, there are established historical practices to cover this. As would be the case for a pedigreed seed producer, a farmer who wishes to maintain some specific genetic characteristic in her or his crop has the responsibility to ensure adequate setback distances to prevent cross-pollination. Seed producers have never been able to sue a neighbouring farmer for allowing pollen to 'pollute' the nature of the seed crop; on the contrary, the responsibility lies with the pedigreed seed producer. Why can organic farmers not accept this precedent that has been established for decades? In any case, cross-pollination of an organic farmer's crop by a neighbouring GM crop would be unlikely to be an issue as farmers usually buy and plant hybrid seeds of crops like maize each planting season. It would become an issue if farmers harvested the seeds produced by cross-pollination with the GM crop in order to plant a new crop, to sell for planting or for feed, or possibly to eat themselves.

Why are organic farmers implacably opposed to GM crops? Could it be because these crops actually pose a threat to their markets? Is it because, in time, we will produce GM crops using fewer chemical fertilisers, pesticides and herbicides, and because these GM crops will not contain the toxic chemicals that organic crops produce to protect themselves from predators and disease? Is it because GM crops will one day have improved nutritional value and other attributes that organic crops will be unable to match? Or is it because GM crops will, in time, be cheaper than their organic counterparts? This is food for thought indeed.

Labelling organic food

The United States Department of Agriculture (USDA) is considering labelling all organically grown products. This could, however, have unintended consequences. A survey conducted on behalf of the National Center for Public Policy Research (http://www.nationalcenter.org/PROganicFood500.html) found that the proposed USDA seal would mislead two-thirds of the public on several key issues:

- 68% said they would interpret a product labeled 'USDA Certified Organic' to be safer to eat than non-organic foods;
- 67% believed 'USDA Certified Organic' to be better than non-organic foods;
- 62% believe 'USDA Certified Organic' to be healthier for consumers than non-organic foods.

'Neither organic nor conventional producers are served by misleading the public over such important issues of food safety and nutrition,' said John Carlisle, director of the Environmental Policy Task Force at the National Center for Public Policy Research (*ibid.*).

According to both the USDA and the leadership of the $6 billion organic industry in the USA, organic certification is only an accreditation of production methods used by farmers and not an assurance of food safety, quality, nutrition or health. Indeed, in a television interview, Katherine DiMatteo, director of the Organic Trade Association in the USA, reiterated that organic products are neither safer nor more nutritious than other food. She noted that organic agriculture is not particularly a food safety claim. But according to the survey, that is not how the public perceives the proposed labels.

A right royal rumpus

In May 2000 Prince Charles used the platform of the prestigious Reith Lecture in the United Kingdom, broadcast by the BBC, to claim that the use of GM technology means that literally nothing is held sacred any more and that scientists are treating the world as a giant laboratory. The Prince, an ardent supporter of organic farming, has long been a vocal critic of 'tinkering' with the genetic make-up of food, raising fears about the impact of GM crops on human health and the environment.

It would appear that the royal household is not unanimous on this subject. The very next month Princess Anne, who is President of the British Association for the Advancement of Science, said in an interview with *The Grocer* magazine that organic food production was not the overall answer. 'Man has been tinkering with food production and plant development for such a long time that it's a bit cheeky to suddenly get nervous about doing it when fundamentally you are doing much the same thing.' The Princess Royal went on to say, 'Life's not simple. But it is a huge oversimplification to say all farming ought to be organic or that there should be no GM foods. I'm sorry – but life isn't that simple. You can add value on the marginal farms through organics. But I feel they are not an overall answer. If you consider things in terms of overall production and sheer weight of numbers, of supporting a population which has so hugely increased, then organics is not the whole answer' (5 June 2000; http://agbioworld.org).

The latest royal to enter the fray is the Duke of Edinburgh. The *Daily Telegraph* reported on Prince Philip's comments, which came as a response to a lecture given at Windsor Castle by the Chief Rabbi, Dr Jonathan Sacks. The Duke is quoted as saying, 'Do not let us forget we have been genetically modifying animals and plants ever since people started selective breeding. People are worried about genetically modified organisms getting into the environment. What people forget is that the introduction of exotic species – like, for instance, the introduction of the grey squirrel into this country – is going to or has done far more damage than a genetically modified piece of potato' (6 June 2000; http://agbioworld.org).

CHAPTER 6: GM CROPS AND FOOD SAFETY

In summary ...

No foodstuffs in the history of humankind have ever been subjected to such an extensive batteries of tests for quality and safety as have foods derived from genetically modified crops. They will continue to be tested on a case-by-case basis and the public can be assured that such foods are safe for human and animal consumption.

While organic foods enjoy a niche market due to their method of production, they should not be seen as 'better', 'safer' or 'healthier'. In fact, organic production may lead to the contamination of food by harmful bacteria. Proponents of GM foods have no problem with organic foods; it is the proponents of organic foods who have a problem with GM foods.

References and further reading

Ames, B. N., Profet, M. and Gold, L. S. (1990) Nature's chemicals and synthetic chemicals: comparative toxicology. *Proceedings of the National Academy of Sciences*, USA. Vol. 87, pp. 7782–7786.

Beever, D. E. and Kemp, C. F. (2000) Safety issues associated with the DNA in animal feed derived from genetically modified crops. *Nutrition Abstracts and Reviews*. Vol. 70, pp. 175–182.

Betz, F. S., Hammond, B. G. and Fuchs, R. S. (2000) Safety and advantages of *Bacillus thuringiensis*-protected plants to control insect pests. *Regulatory Toxicology and Pharmacology*. Vol. 32, pp. 156–173.

Carson, R. (1962) *Silent Spring*. Hamilton, London.

Dingman, D. W. (2000) Growth of *Escherichia coli* O157:H7 in bruised apple (*Malus domestica*) tissue is influenced by cultivar, date of harvest, and source. *Applied and Environmental Microbiology*. Vol. 66, pp. 1077–1083.

Doerfler, W. and Schubbert, R. (1997) Fremde DNA in säugersystem. *Deutsches Ärzteblatt*. Vol. 94, p. 51.

Fenwick, G. R., Heaney, R. K. and Mullin, W. J. (1983) Glucosinolates and their breakdown products in food and food plants. *CRC Critical Reviews of Food Science and Nutrition*. Vol. 18, pp.123–201.

Hammond, B. G., Vicini, J. L., Hartnell, G. F., Naylor, M. W., Knight, C. D., Robinson, E. H., Fuchs, R. L. and Padgette, S. R. (1996) The feeding value of soybeans fed to rats, chickens, catfish and dairy cattle is not altered by genetic incorporation of glyphosate tolerance. *Journal of Nutrition*. Vol. 126, pp. 717–727.

Harrison, L. A., Bailey, M. R., Naylor, M. W., Ream, J. E., Hammond, B. G., Nida, D. L., Burnette, B. L., Nickson, T. E., Mitsdy, T. A., Taylor, M. L., Fuchs, R. L. and Padgette, S. R. (1996) The expressed protein in glyphosate-tolerant soybean, 5-enolpyruvylshikimate-3-phosphate synthase from *Agrobacterium* sp. Strain CP4, is rapidly digested *in vitro* and is not toxic to acutely gavaged mice. *Journal of Nutrition*. Vol. 126, pp.728–740.

Lavrik, P. B., Bartnicki, D. E., Feldman, J., Hammond, B. G., Keck, P. J., Love, S. L., Naylor, M. W., Rogan, G. J., Sims, S. R. and Fuchs, R. L. (1996) Safety assessment of potatoes resistant to Colorado potato beetle. In Engel, K-H., Takeoka, G. R. and Teranishi, R. (eds) *Genetically modified foods: safety issues*. American Chemical Society, Washington.

McClintock, J. T., Schaffer, C. R. and Sjoblad, R. D. (1995) A comparative review of the mammalian toxicity of *Bacillus thuringiensis*-based pesticides. *Pesticide Science*. Vol. 45, pp. 95–105.

McDanell, R., McLean, A. E. M., Hanley, A. B., Heaney, R. K. and Fenwick, G. R. (1988) Chemical and biological properties of indole glucosinolates. *Food and Chemical Toxicology*. Vol. 26, pp. 59–70.

Sanders, P. R., Lee, T. C., Groth, M. E., Astwood, J. D. and Fuchs, R. L. (1998) Safety assessment of insect-protected corn. In: Thomas, J. A. (ed.) *Biotechnology and Safety Assessments*. Second Edition. Taylor and Francis, San Diego, Ca., pp. 241–256.

Shelton, A. M., Tang, J. D., Roush, R. T., Metz, T. D. and Earle, E. D. (2000) Field tests on managing resistance to *Bt*-engineered plants. *Nature Biotechnology*. Vol. 18, pp. 339–342.

Watson, J. C. and Thompson, W. F. (1988) Purification and restriction endonuclease analysis of plant nuclear DNA. In Weissbach, A. and Weissbach, H. (eds) *Methods for Plant Molecular Biology*. p. 57. Academic Press, San Diego.

Ye, X., Al-Babili, S., Klöti, A., Zhang, J., Lucca, P., Beyer, P. and Potrykus, I. (2000) Engineering the provitamin A (ß-carotene) biosynthetic pathway into (carotenoid-free) rice endosperm. *Science*. Vol. 287, pp. 303–305.

Yoshizawa K. and Kishi, S. (1985) Rice in brewing. In: Juliano, B. O. (ed.) *Rice: chemistry and technology*. American Association of Cereal Chemists Inc., St Paul, Minnesota. pp. 619–645.

Chapter 7

Patent or perish

The patent system

In the academic world the dictum is 'publish or perish'. Unless academics produce publications at an acceptable rate, they will not survive in the competitive climate that exists at most academic institutions. In the commercial world the same can be said of patenting. Patents allow inventors to protect their inventions and give them intellectual property rights (IPR), which are complex and contentious.

Supporters of patenting GMOs argue that patenting enables, and indeed drives, large private sector investments into biotechnology research. Both the product (organisms or genes) and the process that led to the development of the product can be patented. Introducing a new product or technology to the marketplace is an expensive investment in time and resources. Patents provide the patent owners legal rights to exclude others from making, using or selling the patented product or process for up to twenty years from the date on which they filed their application for patent protection. Companies, universities, governments and individuals holding patents may license or assign these rights in exchange for royalty payments, license fees or other compensation.

Those wishing to use the patented process may obtain exclusive or non-exclusive licenses from the patent holder. Corporations having the substantial capabilities necessary to develop and market GM seed products consider patents and licenses essential to protect and recoup the considerable expenditures required to bring these new technologies to the marketplace. In plant biotechnology the profits derived from the sale of GM seed are often linked to royalty or technology licence payments to the patent holders. The holder of a patent in a key technology area can issue a license to others who need to use the patented technology for their business. Patent holders expect royalty payments from the use of inventions and therefore generally license their patents to companies that have the enabling infrastructure to successfully bring the product to the market.

Origins of the patent system

The patent system began in England as the practice of the monarch granting royal patents to persons or guilds, giving them exclusive monopoly on an aspect of commerce. However, this system was not based on innovation and was replaced by the Statute of Monopolies in 1623 that eliminated the royal patents and began the incentive theory of patents. The government recognised that giving exclusive rights to certain inventive individuals would tend to confer benefit upon society. This tool was key to the industrialisation of Europe.

In the USA the Constitution provides for laws that promote the progress of science and the useful arts by securing exclusive rights. These rights give individuals the right to exclude others from making, using and selling their inventions without their permission. The system encourages innovation and inventiveness by providing the inventor with this legal reward. The patent system promotes the public disclosure of the invention as opposed to the use of secret process. At the end of the patent term, the invention becomes freely available to the public.

The US Patent and Trademark Office (USPTO) was established in 1836 to examine applications for patents. A similar office was established in England in 1905. Nearly all countries now have patent offices that examine and grant patents. Applications for patents must be applied for in each country individually to protect the invention in that country. It is a challenge for patent applicants seeking international patent protection to work with various national patent offices and within a number of legal frameworks. This has caused some difficulties; for example, in Europe, until 1997, the European Patent Office (EPO) could not patent biological processes and systems.

Patenting plants and other life forms

Prior to 1980, in most countries Plant Breeders' Rights (PBRs) and the Plant Variety Protection Act (PVP) offered protection to plant breeders. These rights safeguard new crop varieties and protect breeders against the resale of seeds they laboured to develop. However, these rights are limited as another plant breeder can still use the seeds as parent material for future developments, and farmers may store seed and sow it the following season. The USPTO Plant Patent Act also protects the work of plant breeders from unauthorised vegetative propagation of their plant varieties.

In an important United States Supreme Court case in 1980, Diamond v. Chakrabarty, the courts decided that a bacterium that Chakrabarty had developed was not a 'product of nature' but rather the result of human intervention, and therefore it could be patented. The patent was awarded to the General Electric Company. The bacterium was a strain of *Pseudomonas* that had been genetically manipulated to digest oil slicks. This was the first test of whether GMOs could be patented. The ruling provided GMOs with protection in the form of utility patents that gave the patent holder access to more powerful laws to protect their inventions (Case: *Diamond v. Chakrabarty* 447 US 303, 1980).

Developing crops with hybrid vigour

In agriculture some important crops, notably maize, are sold as hybrids. Hybrid crop seeds are the products of a cross between two inbred parental lines bred to be uniform and stable but which, themselves, do not produce the desired crop characteristics. The parental lines may contain genes for improved yield, drought resistance, disease resistance, insect resistance or other agriculturally important traits. When the parental lines are crossed to produce hybrid seeds, the hybrid plant expresses all the desired crop traits. So-called 'hybrid vigour' refers to the unique and novel combinations of genes provided by the parents. This vigour is lost if farmers plant the seeds of the hybrid because the genes for the desirable characteristics become segregated in the next generation. In the USA seed companies can patent both the parental inbred lines and the hybrid progeny.

Figure 19 outlines the process of developing hybrid seed. Care has to be taken to prevent self-pollination and ensure that the inbred lines (A and B) do, in fact, cross-pollinate. Therefore, farmers in the seed production business spend considerable time and energy to prevent the lines from self-pollinating. Farmers physically 'emasculate' the female parent to prevent self-pollination. In the case of maize, this labour intensive process involves physically removing the tassles (de-tassling) at the top of the plant that produce the pollen. In most other crops, the anthers must be removed by hand from each flower before the pollen is shed. Methods for producing hybrid seed can also be patented.

Hybrid vigour: the situation whereby the offspring (the hybrid) of two different parental lines is more 'vigorous' (has improved growth traits) than either parent.

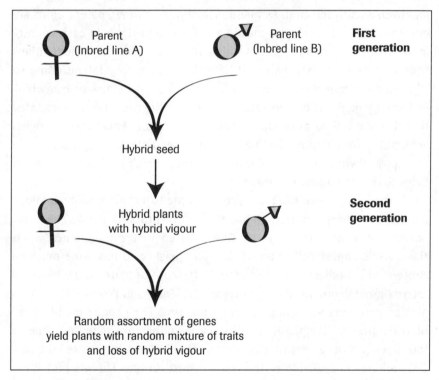

FIGURE 19: The development of hybrid seed.

CHAPTER 7: PATENT OR PERISH

Patenting major crops

The processes used to introduce novel genetic material into crop plants have been patented. Various companies have been assigned these patents, which broadly cover the genetic improvement of particular crops using these methods. For instance, Monsanto Company owns patents for the genetic modification of cotton (US Patent No. 5 004 863) and soybean (US Patent No. 5 015 580).

The non-governmental organisation Rural Advancement Foundation International (RAFI), among others, has challenged these patents. They believe that giving a single corporation monopoly control over the genetic modification of these important crops is contrary to public morality. RAFI proposes that this could represent a threat to world security. They are concerned that a corporation may secure such a dominant patent position with regard to a crop that it could exclude all others from making genetic improvements to the crop. As mentioned above, however, patent rights are not universal and developers must apply for patent rights in each country individually. Furthermore, patent rights allow the holder to exclude others from profiting from the patented invention only if they intend doing so without the permission of the patent holder. Patent holders of many bio-technology methods or agriculturally important genes have demonstrated that they are willing to provide licenses for their use. Finally, patent rights are granted for a limited time period and many biotechnology patents will be expiring within the next five to ten years, which is about the time it takes to develop a new GM variety.

Organisations like RAFI are also concerned that plant biotechnology patents put germplasm from public research institutions at risk. The International Rice Research Institute (IRRI), based in the Philippines, holds the world's largest collection of rice germplasm and has done much to conserve the biodiversity of this crop. In the case of maize and wheat, the International Centre for the Improvement of Maize and Wheat (CIMMYT) in Mexico conserves vast amounts of germplasm. The genetic modification of these public germplasm varieties, by introducing a patented gene or introducing a gene using a patented method, potentially makes the new GM varieties unavailable to the research institutions. Patents protecting GM varieties do not affect the unmodified variety or its use. However, producers of new GM varieties should ensure that research institutions like IRRI and CIMMYT derive benefit from making original germplasm available for genetic modification. Biotechnology companies could, for example, enter into profit-sharing agreements with the research institutions.

Companies holding patents on genes and processes or methods are entering into cross-licensing agreements for the use and development of these inventions in GM crops. Thus the technology is becoming more broadly available as companies with the necessary expertise and resources to develop and market new GM seeds make these methods and products available. Most of the smaller seed companies in developed countries have entered into license agreements with patent holders and produce their own varieties with the improved genetic traits.

The laws covering utility patents on foreign genes and biotechnology methods used in GM varieties permit the patent owner to exclude farmers from saving the seed for future use. In contrast, the Plant Variety Protection Act only prevent farmers from selling the seed to others. As a result, farmers who buy certain patented GM seeds enter into an agreement with the company selling them. This might include the farmer agreeing not to save or sell seed. In return the company guarantees trait performance and technical support that could include helping to market the farmer's crop.

While some may argue that this gives the company too much control over the farmer, others reply that market forces will prevail. If the cost of buying the seed and entering into an agreement outweighs the benefits derived from the GM seeds, the farmers do not have to buy them. No one forces farmers to buy GM seeds – they will do so if the profits are sufficiently attractive. Just as a software developer or a music company has the right to insist that buyers of their products do not copy them illegally, so seed companies have the right to prevent their products from being reproduced illegally. They have the right to reap the rewards of their investments; and there will only be rewards for as long as farmers continue to find their products attractive.

CHAPTER 7: PATENT OR PERISH

The effect of patents on the developing world

Threats to the developing world

In contrast to the private companies that have driven the development of GM crops in the developed countries, public investment is driving GM technology in developing countries. Most of the products generated in developing countries, including those from centres within the Consultative Group for International Agricultural Research (CGIAR), such as IRRI and CIMMYT, are considered to be in the public domain and available to all.

The largest germplasm collections of crops important to developing countries are held in trust at CGIAR centres. Currently, most of the benefits of agricultural biotechnology are being realised by developed countries where patent protection and regulatory infrastructure are in place. Some say that this neglects the needs of poor countries. Ismail Serageldin, the past Chair of CGIAR, has coined the phrase 'scientific apartheid' to describe this phenomenon (Serageldin, 1999, p. 389), which could further marginalise the developing world. He proposes that a solution may lie in establishing more precise domains of intellectual property.

Serageldin claims that the patenting of both processes and products is seriously undermining the ability of public sector enterprises such a CGIAR to access knowledge and technology. However, patent laws in the USA and many other countries allow non-profit organisations to use the information and methods disclosed in patent material for research purposes. As these organisations develop products that are useful in developing countries, agreements will need to be made to protect the rights of patent owners and ensure continued research and development of new GM crops.

Private sector companies should be allowed to patent the products they develop and wish to sell. The technology is not only expensive to develop but requires a high level of technical skill and infrastructure, more than is necessary for classical crop breeding programmes. However, some imaginative thinking is required in order to circumvent the problems of lack of accessibility to poor countries. The private sector needs incentives to form partnerships with developing countries to research and provide modified crops important to their subsistence farming economies. 'Orphan crops' such as millet, cassava, and sorghum are of little interest to the western world but could make the difference between life and death to the people of Africa.

Progressive partnerships

There is some progress, however; for example Monsanto and Zeneca have decided to provide, free of royalties, their technology for virus resistance and delayed ripening of papayas, developed by a consortium of five Southeast Asian countries (Thailand, Malaysia, Philippines, Indonesia and Vietnam). The consortium agreed to the following conditions (Hautea et al., 1999):

- to use the technologies only in papaya;
- to use the technologies under approved bio-safety regulations;
- to consume the transformed papaya within the five-country consortium only.

Another example is an agreement between Monsanto and the Kenyan Agricultural Research Institute (KARI), which provided technology royalty-free for KARI to develop and distribute virus-resistant sweet potatoes in Africa. Monsanto trained numerous Kenyan research scientists and provided expertise and technical support for the production, selection and field testing of transgenic sweet potato plants containing a gene to control sweet potato feather mottle virus (Qaim, 1999).

Yet another good example of collaboration between the private and public sector is that of virus-resistant potatoes in Mexico. Monsanto entered into an agreement with the Centre for Research and Advanced Studies (CINVESTAV) in 1991 to train their research scientists in plant molecular biology, virus resistance analysis and genetic transformation of potato (Qaim, 1998). In this effort, Monsanto donated:

- patented coat protein genes (see Chapter 3) for resistance to potato virus X (PVX) and potato virus Y (PVY);
- patented replicase gene for potato leaf-roll virus (PLRV) resistance;
- the patented genetic element controlling the expression of these genes in potato.

Scientists from CINVESTAV carried out the transfer of the genes in Mexico in 1992 and the first field trial occurred in 1993. Subsequently they transformed different potato varieties and conducted multi-location field trials with three different varieties. Although Monsanto was the primary technical collaborator in these projects, academic scientists, the International

CHAPTER 7: PATENT OR PERISH

Service for the Acquisition of Agri-Biotech Applications (ISAAA), the Rockefeller Foundation and USAID, the United States international aid agency, also made technical contributions. Facilitation by external scientists and not-for-profit institutions were critical in moving these projects forward.

These partnerships appear to be working well but they are few in number. We need new and more comprehensive collaborations between the public and private sectors that respect IPR protection in order to ensure a win-win situation that includes the poor. In a paper in the journal *Nature*, Gordon Conway, President of the Rockefeller Foundation, and Gary Toenniessen (1999) argue that the cost of accomplishing this will be significant but should not be excessive. They cite the example of Rockefeller Foundation funding of rice biotechnology research over the past 15 years. With funding of US$100 million they have trained over 400 scientists from Asia, Africa and Latin America. In several places in Asia there is now a critical mass of talented scientists who are applying the new tools of biotechnology to rice improvement.

Opportunities for collaboration

Why did Monsanto donate virus resistance technology to Mexico, Kenya and Southeast Asia? What was in it for them? Perhaps they wished to improve their image as a 'responsible global citizen' against the backdrop of North-South inequalities and food insecurity in the Third World? The cynic might say that this particular public relations exercise did not cost Monsanto very much as it was confined to Mexican varieties of potatoes and not to any imported ones. The scientists at Monsanto believe that agricultural improvements, such as virus resistance, will have a big impact on the yield potential of subsistence crops in the developing world. Crop biotechnology has the potential to benefit resource-poor farmers even more than large-scale farmers and Monsanto states that they are committed to enabling the use of this technology in developing countries.

Gordon Conway, in an address to Monsanto on 24 June 1999 (http://www.biotech-info.net/gordon_conway.html), suggested that, with little competitive loss, the big seed companies could agree to use the plant variety protection (PVP) system in developing countries. They would do this in cooperation with public breeding agencies, rather than relying on the use

114 –

of patents to protect their crops. PVP allows farmers to save seed for their own re-use. It also allows plant breeders to use seed in research designed to produce further varietal improvements.

Conway also urged major companies to become involved in training personnel in developing countries in the science and management of bio-technology, IPR, biosafety and international negotiations. He believes that governments and the public in developing countries will be more receptive to the new technologies if they know that their own scientists and regula-tory authorities thoroughly understand it, are able to use it and have in place biosafety protocols designed to minimise risks.

This is certainly true of a number of countries in sub-Saharan Africa. In March 2000 at a meeting in Mombasa, Kenya, convened by the African Centre for Technology Studies, it came to light that the only African countries with legislation in place to handle GM crops were South Africa, Zimbabwe and Kenya. Some other countries, such as Zambia, have *ad hoc* arrangements for dealing with applications for field trials of GM crops.

On the question of licensing, Conway suggested that companies with IPR to certain techniques or materials that could benefit developing countries might agree to license these at no cost. Conway and Toennissen (1999) concede that the days of unencumbered, free exchange of plant genetic materials are over. We need agreements and procedures to ensure that public sector institutions have access to the technological and genetic resources needed to produce improved crop varieties for farmers in devel-oping countries. If multinationals wish to find a receptive and growing market in developing countries, they will need to work with the public sector to make sure this happens.

In April 2000, the Japanese Minister of Agriculture, Fisheries and Forestry announced, on behalf of the International Rice Genome Sequen-cing Project (IRGSP), that Monsanto was making available its draft rice genome sequence in order to accelerate decoding of the entire rice genome (http://www.monsanto.com/monsanto/mediacenter/2000/00apr4_rice.html). Monsanto also made the draft data available to researchers outside the IRGSP at no cost, through the website http://www.rice-research.org. They encourage users of the data to make the results of their research available widely. However, there is a *quid pro quo*. In the event that researchers do file patent applications based on the use of Monsanto's sequence data,

CHAPTER 7: PATENT OR PERISH

they agree to give the company an early opportunity to negotiate for a non-exclusive license to such patents. The company must also be prepared to pay royalties to the inventors. This may prove to be an example of how a private company can broadly share data it has produced internally in order to improve agriculture without compromising its commercial interests.

In summary ...

Patents are one way of protecting a developer's rights to a return on their investment in developing a GM crop. Patents allow these technologies and products to be used, controlled by a system of royalties or licenses for a given period of time. In order for agricultural biotechnology to be applied in developing countries, we will need more public-private sector partnerships, facilitated by not-for-profit organisations.

References and further reading

Hautea R., Chan, Y. K., Attathom, S. and Krattiger, A. F. (1999) The papaya biotechnology network of Southeast Asia: biosafety considerations and papaya background information. *ISAAA Briefs*. No. 11. ISAAA, Ithaca, N.Y.

Qaim, M. (1998) Transgenic virus resistant potatoes in Mexico: potential socioeconomic implications for North-South biotechnology transfer. *ISAAA Briefs*. No. 7. ISAAA, Ithaca, N.Y.

Qaim, M. (1999) The economic effects of genetically modified orphan commodities: projections for sweet potato in Kenya. *ISAAA Briefs*. No. 13. ISAAA, Ithaca, N.Y.

Conway, G. and Toenniessen, G. (1999) Feeding the world in the twenty-first century. *Nature*. Vol. 401, pp. C55–C58.

Serageldin, I. (1999) Biotechnology and food security in the twenty-first century. *Science*. Vol. 285, pp. 387–389.

FIGURE 1:
Plant breeding over centuries has resulted in a number of varieties of maize that differ in the size and shape of the cobs and the colour of the kernels.
(Source: Van Rensburg, undated)

FIGURE 2: The structure of DNA, showing how the double helix replicates itself.

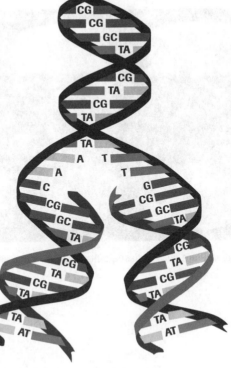

FIGURE 4: Plant cells in tissue culture (A) produce shoots and roots (B).

FIGURE 6A: The Biolistic® Accell® gene gun.

FIGURE 6B: A transgenic maize plant resistant to the herbicide Bialaphos together with a non-transgenic plant. Both were sprayed with Bialaphos.

FIGURE 8: The effects of the Colorado potato beetle on (A) a potato plant, (B) a field of non-*Bt* potatoes and (C) a field of *Bt* potatoes. *(Source: Kenneth Palmer)*

FIGURE 10: The monarch butterfly.

FIGURE 13A: A healthy cassava plant.

FIGURE 13B: A cassava plant infected with cassava mosaic virus.

FIGURE 15: Flavr Savr™ tomatoes have many desirable characteristics compared with ordinary tomatoes.

Ordinary tomato

Flavr Savr™ tomato

TRANSGENIC PLANTS
Trial Release

FIGURE 20: Infruitec in Stellenbosch, South Africa, undertook a fenced field trial of herbicide-resistant strawberries.

FIGURE 21A: Before spraying, the herbicide-resistant strawberries are hidden by weeds.

FIGURE 21B: After spraying the dead weeds act as a mulch.

FIGURE 24: The effects of maize streak virus on a maize plant (A) and on the growth of the maize crop (B).

Chapter 8

The agriculture police

Regulation and monitoring in South Africa

The South African Committee for Genetic Experimentation

The South African Committee for Genetic Experimentation (SAGENE) was established in the late 1970s when genetic engineering first began. It developed guidelines initially for the safe use of GM bacteria in laboratories and, more recently, for work with all GMOs, including plants. The following bodies nominated members:

- the statutory councils (the Agricultural Research Council, Council for Scientific and Industrial Research, Foundation for Research Development and the Medical Research Council);
- the Department of National Health and Population Development;
- the Department of Environmental Affairs and Tourism;
- the Committee of University Principals;
- the Southern African Institute of Ecologists and Environmental Scientists;
- the Industrial Biotechnology Association of Southern Africa.

SAGENE also had as a member a legal representative with knowledge of environmental issues. Most, but not all, of the members these bodies nominated had a working knowledge of genetic engineering.

For many years the committee dealt with all requests for permission to carry out laboratory, glasshouse or field trials with GMOs. However, as the volume of work increased, *ad hoc* sub-committees consisting jointly of SAGENE members and outside experts handled requests. Applicants had to comply with a voluntary code of conduct but SAGENE was simply an advisory body having no 'teeth' to enforce compliance. As most of the applications for trials dealt with plant material, SAGENE's role was to advise the Department of Agriculture regarding the merits of each application.

The Department laid down and monitored the conditions under which trials were conducted.

An amusing example of these conditions comes to mind. One of the earliest applications was in 1990 for a field trial of herbicide-resistant cotton in KwaZulu-Natal. SAGENE recommended that the trial proceed but the Department of Agriculture decided that the trial area must be fenced off with a lockable gate. As the area was fairly large, the cost of fencing was considerable. Accordingly, the company involved appealed against this ruling, citing the fact that public interest in such a fenced-off field would be far greater than in an ordinary field and could result in people, particularly inquisitive children, climbing over the fence to investigate further. As this was undesirable from a GM-safety point of view, SAGENE supported the appeal. However, the Department took some convincing. It was only when the company applied for a second, similar trial that the Department of Agriculture relented on the fencing requirement. Note also that, before SAGENE approved any trial, it required the company or institute involved to embark upon a public awareness campaign to inform residents and farmers in the area of the up-coming trial. This requirement is now embedded in the GMO Act, No. 15 of 1997.[1]

Research institutes could afford to fence off smaller trials, such as trials of herbicide-tolerant strawberries conducted at the Agricultural Research Council's Infruitec centre in Stellenbosch (see Figure 20 on page 122 in the colour section). This was the first trial of a GM crop developed in South Africa (Du Plessis *et al.*, 1995).

Figure 21 (see page 123 in the colour section) shows how effective this herbicide resistance in strawberries proved to be. Before spraying, Figure 21A shows the strawberries almost completely hidden by weeds. After spraying (Figure 21B) the dead weeds act as a mulch to protect the plants from the hot, dry conditions that prevail in the Western Cape during the summer growing season.

The GMO Act

SAGENE received numerous applications between 1990 and November 2000 (see Figures 25 and 26 in Chapter 10). In theory, SAGENE's role came to an end on 23 May 1997 when Parliament passed the Genetically Modified

Organisms (GMO) Act. In practice, SAGENE continued to act, albeit on an *ad hoc* basis, until mid-1999 when a new administrative structure took over.

At that time, SAGENE recommended that the government departments involved in monitoring GMOs nominate the members of the new Executive Council. This Council appoints an Advisory Committee and a Registrar and is the body that formally approves trials or commercial releases. SAGENE was afraid that an Executive Council consisting of civil servants would slow down the approval process. However, politicians saw the situation differently. Consequently, the present Executive Council consists of officers from six government departments (Agriculture; Arts, Culture, Science and Technology; Environmental Affairs and Tourism; Health; Trade and Industry; and Labour). The Executive Council only held its first meeting late in 1999 when the Registrar was appointed. The Advisory Committee was eventually appointed in February 2000. The current Registrar is Shadrack Moephuli of the Genetic Resources Directorate of the Department of Agriculture. Figure 22 shows the bureaucratic structure responsible for upholding the GMO Act.

FIGURE 22: Structure of the Executive Council, Registrar and Advisory Committee established to uphold the GMO Act.

CHAPTER 8: THE AGRICULTURE POLICE

The powers and duties of the Executive Council include:

- deciding on the issue of permits to undertake glasshouse and field trials or commercial releases of GM crops and other GMOs;
- overseeing the office of the Registrar;
- liaison with other countries, especially neighbouring countries;
- advising the Minister of Agriculture;
- ensuring law enforcement according to the GMO Act.

The Registrar's duties include:

- administration of the Act;
- issuing permits;
- being pro-active in terms of contravention of the Act (which can result in fines and imprisonment);
- appointing inspectors to monitor field trials;
- ensuring compliance with the conditions of permits.

The Advisory Committee consists of up to eight members knowledgeable in the field of GMOs and two persons from the public sector with knowledge of ecology and GMOs. Their functions include:

- advising the Minister of Agriculture and the Executive Council on environmental impacts related to the introduction of GMOs;
- consideration of all matters pertaining to the contained use, import and export of GMOs;
- consideration of all matters regarding regulations and guidelines;
- liaison with international groups working in similar areas;
- obtaining outside input and information on any issue about which they lack competency.

The Registrar appoints field inspectors to ensure that trials are carried out in accordance with the Act. In addition to routine inspections of all field trials, an inspector may obtain a warrant from the local magistrate to conduct an investigation at any place to ensure compliance with all provisions of the Act.

The people who carry out the field trials are responsible for implementing measures to avoid adverse impacts on the environment. The permit holders are liable for any damage caused by GMOs.

Regulations of the GMO Act[2] state that:

- A permit is required to import, export, develop, use or release GMOs.
- Academic and research facilities are exempt from the permit requirement for certain activities but must be registered with the Registrar. All researchers are required to conduct a risk assessment of projects; records of these must be maintained at the facility.
- Time frames for applications, the information that is required and the fees involved must be provided.
- The applicant is responsible for notifying the public of trial and general releases of GMOs. The applicant must place a notice in three different newspapers in the area and submit copies to the Registrar with the relevant application. The Registrar receives any comments or objections and refers these to the Executive Council, which decides on a course of action.
- People carrying out field trials must take measures to avoid accidents and must report any accidents immediately to the Registrar.
- There must be effective waste management to prevent negative impacts on the environment or human and animal health.

Figure 23 illustrates the process that follows once the Registrar for Genetic Resources receives an application:

- The Registrar appoints a member of the Advisory Committee to act as chair for the review.
- The Review Chair appoints a sub-committee of three reviewers who are not members of the Advisory Committee.
- The Review Chair receives reports from the sub-committee and compiles a report for the Registrar.
- The Registrar submits this report to all members of the Advisory Committee for comment.
- The Advisory Committee reaches a decision and informs the Registrar.
- The Registrar presents a letter of recommendation to the Executive Council, which finally approves or rejects the application.

The GMO regulations stipulate that this process should take no longer than 90 days for a decision on field trials and 180 days for a decision on general release applications. All reviewers and members of the Executive Council and Advisory Committee sign a deed of confidentiality.

CHAPTER 8: THE AGRICULTURE POLICE

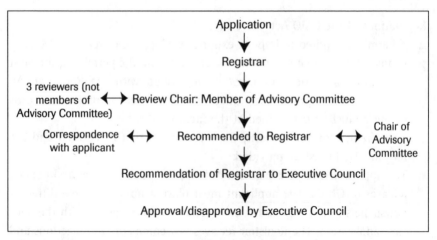

FIGURE 23: The process followed when the Registrar for Genetic Resources receives an application for trial or commercial release of a GMO.

Each application is reviewed on a case-by-case basis, but it is possible to 'fast-track' the process in the case of applications for second or third trials of the same crop. The reviewers take a number of issues into account when assessing an application for a field trial. The applicant is responsible for addressing these issues:

■ What is the potential for toxic or allergic responses in humans or animals?
■ How stable is the introduced gene?
■ What is the potential that the plant may exhibit pathogenic properties?
■ Can the crop cause damage to agricultural commodities?
■ What is the likelihood of the plant becoming weedy, compared to traditional varieties?
■ Can the introduced gene be transferred to sexually compatible plants, and if so what could the consequences of such a transfer be?
■ In the case of insect- or disease-resistant plants, what effects could the transferred gene have on non-target organisms?
■ What impacts could the plants have on agricultural practices, including Integrated Pest Management (IPM) and resistance management?

Table 4 shows an example of a bio-safety risk assessment prepared by the reviewers.

Food Safety	Finding
Metabolic and physical changes in plant	None
Expression levels of the introduced gene in plant during the different growth stages	Low expression (less than 0.001% of total protein)
Foreign protein levels in food grade oil and feed cake derived from cotton seeds	None in oil, low (less than 0.001% of total protein) in cake
Toxicity	Toxic to lepidopteran insects, i.e. the target insects
Allergenicity	No evidence
Changes in nutrition and composition	Substantially equivalent to unmodified cotton
Changes in digestibility and digestion products	None
Foreign protein activity in consumers and processed oils/feeds	None
Unexpected products	None
Stability of the introduced gene	Stable for seven generations in SA and longer in the USA and Australia
Environmental Impact	**Finding**
Spread of gene (pollen, seed or vegetative propagation)	No negative impact
Out-crossing to weeds or natural flora	No compatible local relatives; not invasive
Effect on insects, birds and other consumers	Only lepidopterans affected; renews biodiversity (insects and birds) in and around crops due to reduced use of insecticides
Effect on sustainable agriculture	Positive; less input and 'peace of mind' management
Effect on soil, water and air	Positive; less pesticide load
Socio-economic effects	Benefits rural, small-scale farmers
Stability	Stable for 10 years worldwide
Other specific concerns, e.g. development of insect resistance	Compulsory integrated pest management to minimise development of resistance

TABLE 4: Bio-safety risk assessment of *Bt* cotton in South Africa. *(Source: Innovation Biotechnology, 2000)*

Reaction to GMOs

While South Africa was developing GMO legislation and regulatory systems, Europe had erupted in an anti-GM food frenzy. The reasons for this are complex and I deal with them in Chapters 5, 6 and 10. An article in *The Economist* of 19 June 1999 entitled 'Who's afraid of genetically modified foods?' made this amusing comment, 'If the current British furore over genetically modified foods were a crop not a crisis, you can bet Monsanto or its competitors would have patented it. It has many of the traits that genetic engineers prize: it is incredibly fertile, thrives in inhospitable conditions, has tremendous consumer appeal and is easy to cross with other interests to create a hardy new hybrid. Moreover, it seems to resist anything that might kill it, from scientific evidence to official reassurance.'

The GM food debate soon began in South Africa, although the issues differed markedly from those in the Northern Hemisphere (see Chapter 10). In July 1999 at the Southern African Economic Summit the Minister of Agriculture, Thoko Didiza, came out openly in support of GM crops for sustainable agriculture in South Africa. Of course, no one is saying that we have all the answers. Scientists support research that continues to investigate aspects of concern.

International regulation and monitoring

Regulatory authorities in the USA

In the USA, the US Department of Agriculture (USDA), the Food and Drug Administration (FDA) and the Environmental Protection Agency (EPA) are involved in regulating GMOs. These bodies support a programme of competitively awarded, peer-reviewed research grants focusing on current and future safety issues to expand the existing body of knowledge regarding crops and food derived from biotechnology.

The Food, Drug and Cosmetic Act gives the FDA sweeping authority to regulate the safety of all foods, including GM foods. The Act permits the FDA to remove any harmful product from store shelves at any time and to criminally prosecute its manufacturer. The FDA considers a wide range of factors during the consultative process, including their safety, nutritional value and potential allergic and toxic effects. Manufacturers test products extensively in order to meet their legal obligation to ensure the safety of food; for example, one strain of GM soybean has been subjected to 1 800 analyses (http://www.whybiotech.com).

The EPA and the USDA also strictly regulate GM crops. The EPA regulates pest- and insect-resistant crops and the USDA oversees field and agricultural environmental testing of all GM crops. Let us look at the steps involved in approval of a GM crop in the USA. The USDA:

- must give formal approval for field trials to be conducted;
- must give authority for the developer to ship seeds from the greenhouse to field trial sites;
- spends nearly a year reviewing a full package of field trials and studies.

If the new plant performs a function traditionally performed by a chemical pesticide, for instance insect-resistant maize or cotton, the EPA:

- must grant an experimental use permit if the developer wants to test 10 acres or more;
- must decide whether limits (tolerances) should be set on the amount of pest-control protein in foods derived from the crop;
- spends about 18 months reviewing a host of environmental and toxicological studies.

The FDA is involved in the process almost from the beginning and is the primary overseer of food safety. The FDA:

- meets with the developer early in the process and provides guidelines on what studies it considers appropriate to ensure food and feed safety;
- interacts with the developer over several years;
- has the authority, under the Food, Drug and Cosmetic Act, to remove immediately from the market any food it deems to be unsafe.

During the above process the three federal agencies examine health and environmental safety. The USDA, over years of field trials, examines many parameters of the GM crop to determine whether inserting a new gene will cause the plant to differ from its conventionally bred counterpart in any aspect other than the introduced trait. The field trials also tell the USDA whether the crop will have any effect on non-target species, such as in the case of insect resistance. The USDA is also responsible for ensuring that the plant will not become, or create, a weedy pest.

The EPA reviews toxicological studies to ensure that the new crop does not harm animals or humans. In the process, researchers feed high doses of the introduced protein to rodents, beneficial insects, birds and fish. Digestibility studies and other data determine if the inserted gene results in the production of an allergen.

The FDA compares the significant parameters of the improved plant with its traditional counterpart, including agronomic and physiological characteristics and nutritional components (such as protein, starch, sugar, fat and amino acids). Any unexpected changes lead to further studies. The FDA assesses the safety of any newly expressed protein other than those which are pesticidal and hence the responsibility of the EPA. The FDA also assesses consumption levels and any potential impacts on human or animal nutrition. If the FDA detects no changes, they can conclude with great assurance that the GM crop is as safe as the conventional crop.

Despite all these regulatory protocols, on 3 May 2000 the Clinton Administration announced a wide-ranging assessment of federal environmental and food safety regulations regarding agricultural biotechnology. The intent of the assessment was to strengthen the scientific basis for regulations and to improve consumer access to information on food products. For instance, the FDA will propose a rule to ensure that companies inform them at least 120 days before they introduce GM crops, food products or animal feeds onto the market. This new rule will replace the current voluntary practice of consulting with the agency. The FDA will also develop guidelines for labelling foods to indicate whether or not they contain GM ingredients. The USDA will work with farmers and industry to develop reliable testing procedures and quality assurance programmes for differentiating GM from unmodified commodities. The USDA, FDA and EPA will support an expanded programme of competitive grants focusing on bio-safety issues (Hallerman, 2000).

The response to this announcement has been mixed. A particularly strident attack came in a letter to the Editor of *The Wall Street Journal* headed 'Regulatory gangs maul biotech' (H. Miller, personal communication, 2000). The author claimed that the USDA had carried out experiments with gene-spliced plants that were ten- to twenty-fold more expensive than the same field trials with virtually identical organisms using older, less precise techniques. Miller, on the other hand, believes that the USDA is 'gagging' biotechnology with excessive regulation. Time will tell whether the new procedures will help or hinder the development of GM crops.

Regulatory authorities: comparing Europe with the USA

Any author deciding to write a book on GM crops and foods is bound to be asked the question, 'How will you know when to stop?' This is such a rapidly developing field, both scientifically and socio-economically, that inevitably much of what appears in this book will be out of date by the time it is published. And possibly, the chapter most at risk is this one.

Compare Europe and America for example. European Union Environment Ministers, under public pressure to get tough on GMOs, agreed on 24 June 1999 to suspend authorisation of new hi-tech crops and foods until 2002 when a new law on licensing the products is expected to come into force.

The situation is very different in the USA. Here are some excerpts from a speech given by the Agriculture Secretary, Dan Glickman to the National Press Club.[3] 'Agricultural biotechnology has enormous potential to help combat hunger. GM plants have the potential to resist killer weeds that are, literally, starving people in Africa and other parts of the developing world. Biotechnology can help us solve some of the most vexing environmental problems: it could reduce pesticide use, increase yields, improve nutritional content, and use less water. We're employing bio-engineered fungi to remove ink from pulp in a more environmentally sensitive manner. But, as with any new technology, the road is not always smooth. Right now, in some parts of the world there is great consumer resistance and great cynicism toward biotechnology. In Europe protesters have torn up test plots of biotechnology-derived crops and some of the major food companies in Europe have stopped using GMOs in their products.'

He then adds a note of caution. 'Now, more than ever, with these technologies in their relative infancy, I think it's important that, as we encourage the development of these new food-production systems, we cannot blindly embrace their benefits. We have to ensure public confidence in general, consumer confidence in particular, and assure farmers the knowledge that they will benefit.'

Then on a note of encouragement, 'The important question is not, do we accept the changes the biotechnology revolution can bring, but are we willing to heed the lessons of the past in helping us to harness this burgeoning technology? The promise and potential are enormous, but so too are the questions, many of which are completely legitimate. Today, on the threshold of this revolution, we have to grapple with and satisfy those questions so we can in fact fulfil biotechnology's awesome potential.'

'To this end, today I am laying out five principles I believe should guide us in our approach to biotechnology in the twenty-first century. They are:

1. An arm's length regulatory process: Government regulators must continue to stay an arm's length, dispassionate distance from the companies developing and promoting these products, and continue to protect public health, safety and the environment.

2. Consumer acceptance: Consumer acceptance is fundamentally based on an arm's length regulatory process. There may be a role for information labelling, but fundamental questions to acceptance will depend on sound regulation.

3. Fairness to farmers: Biotechnology has to result in greater, not fewer options for farmers. The industry has to develop products that show real, meaningful results for farmers, particularly small- and medium-size family farmers.

4. Corporate citizenship: In addition to their desire for profit, biotechnology companies must also understand and respect the role of the arm's length regulator, the farmer and the consumer.

5. Free and open trade: We cannot let others hide behind unfounded, unwarranted scientific claims to block commerce in agriculture.'

Secretary Glickman concluded by saying, 'We need to examine all of our laws and policies to ensure that, in the rush to bring biotech products to the market, small and medium farmers are not simply plowed under. We will need to integrate issues like privatisation of genetic resources, patent holders' rights and public research to see if our approach is helping or harming the public good and family farmers. It is not the government who harnesses the power of the airwaves, but it is the government who regulates it. That same principle might come to apply to discoveries in nature as well. And that debate is just getting started.'

Gaskell *et al.* (1999) have investigated the differences in public perceptions of five applications of modern biotechnology, looking for explanations for the differences between Europe and the USA. They point out that in an increasingly complex world, trust functions as a substitute for knowledge. Europe and the USA have rather different histories of biotechnology regulation. In the USA a relatively short, but very active and often volatile, public debate settled most of the key regulatory issues regarding genetic engineering by the end of the 1980s. Regulators did not consider that biotechnology posed a special risk and regulation was contained within existing laws that addressed known physical risks of new products. In Europe, on the other hand, a relatively protracted public debate has yet to achieve a viable consensus. European regulators have dealt with biotechnology as a novel process requiring novel regulatory provisions.

Surveys in Europe and the USA asked questions concerning trust in regulation and regulatory bodies. Although Europeans showed confidence in the United Nations and the World Health Organisation, when asked about their level of confidence in being told the truth about GM crops, their votes went to environmental (23%), consumer (16%) and farming (16%) organisations. At only 4% of the vote, national public bodies commanded very little support indeed. In the USA, by contrast, the USDA carried the support of 90% of respondents and the FDA 84%. Trust in regulatory authorities is far higher in the USA than in Europe (*ibid.*).

Another difference between the USA and Europe lies in public perceptions. A survey asked participants three True/False questions to test their perceptions of food biotechnology. These were:

■ Ordinary tomatoes do not contain genes while genetically modified tomatoes do.
■ By eating a genetically modified fruit a person's genes could become modified.
■ Genetically modified animals are always bigger than ordinary ones.

Naturally the answers to all three questions are False. Significantly more people in the USA than in Europe recognised this. 'If more Europeans think that GM foods are the only foods containing genes, that eating GM foods may result in genetic infection, and that GM animals are always bigger, it is hardly surprising that they approach modern food biotechnology with greater suspicion' (*ibid.*, p. 386).

The greater prevalence of menacing food images in Europe may well be related to recent food safety scares such as bovine spongiform encephalopathy (BSE) or 'mad cow disease'. These scares have sensitised large sections of the European public to potential dangers inherent in industrial farming practices and the lack of effective regulatory oversight. Also, Europeans tend to view farmland as an important environmental resource and generally live closer to agricultural lands than Americans do. In the USA less than 2% of the population lives and works on farms, which are usually situated far away from where the other 98% of the population lives.

It is clear that trust in regulatory authorities is considerably higher in the USA than in Europe. This may help to explain why public concern is so much greater in Europe than in the United States.

Europe may be changing its mind, however. In an article in *Lancet*, Birchard (2000, p. 320) states that 'The European Commission is moving to end its unofficial 18-month moratorium on genetically modified (GM) foods, indicating that they believe the time has come to accept that GM foods do not pose a serious threat to public health.'

The precautionary principle

Most definitions of the precautionary principle fall into two broad classes:
1. The strong precautionary principle: take no action unless you are certain that it will do no harm;
2. The weak precautionary principle: lack of full certainty is no justification for preventing an action that might be harmful.

Governments have generally employed the weak precautionary principle, while environmental and consumer organisations have typically employed the strong precautionary principle. Unfortunately, demanding that a technology should not be permitted until it has been proven to be harmless is equivalent to requiring an infinitely high standard of proof, which can never be achieved. In its strong form, the precautionary principle encourages taking a hyper-cautious approach to change. This means imposing very strict controls on the approval of new technologies.

Many countries base their regulations on the strong precautionary principle. They frequently rationalise their rules on the basis that regulatory action should be taken to avoid a risk, even when there is incomplete scientific evidence as to the existence or magnitude of such risk. In practice, this has been interpreted to mean that a technology should not be used unless and until it has been shown to be absolutely safe. This means that the usual burden of proof is reversed. New technologies are assumed to be guilty until their innocence is proven to a standard demanded by their critics. In most cases this is a practical impossibility. The strong precautionary principle can never be satisfied as long as there is an inventive alarmist who can think of yet one more possible risk that has not yet been absolutely disproved.

Elizabeth M. Whelan, president of the American Council on Science and Health, aptly sums up the shortcomings of the precautionary principle. First, it always assumes worst-case scenarios. Second, it distracts consumers and policy makers alike from the known and proven threats to human health. Third, it assumes no health detriment from the proposed regulations and restrictions. In other words, the precautionary principle overlooks the possibility that real public health risks can be associated with expending resources on eliminating miniscule, hypothetical risks associated with genetically engineered crops and foods. What are the costs associated with not embracing GM crops (Miller, 2000)?

Is the precautionary principle a tool that countries such as those in Europe can use to prevent imports from countries growing GM crops, such as America and, in due course, developing countries? Is the whole anti-GM movement in Europe nothing other than a trade war? The precautionary principle provides ample opportunity for protectionism-minded politicians to thwart competition and extract concessions from biotechnology companies. Under this new standard of evidence, which European officials have warmly embraced and implemented, regulatory bodies are free to withhold approvals arbitrarily and indefinitely.

In a thought provoking article by Robert Paarlberg (2000) the author states, 'The international debate over GM crops pits a cautious, consumer-driven Europe against aggressive American industry. Yet the real stake-holders in this debate are poor farmers and poorly fed consumers in Asia, Africa, and Latin America.'

The Nuffield Council on Bio-ethics in the United Kingdom announced in May 1999 that GM foods are safe for consumption. European consumers, distrustful since the 1996 outbreak of 'mad cow disease', discounted these reassurances. Although this disease has nothing to do with genetic modification, it generated new consumer anxieties about food safety at precisely the moment when US-grown GM soybeans were first being cleared for import into the European Union. A number of third parties, including non-governmental organisations (NGOs), quickly stepped into the fray to exploit these anxieties. Their well-publicised campaigns forced significant corporate and government concessions in Europe. In April 1998, without scientific evidence that GM foods cause any harm, Brussels stopped approving new GM crops for use in or import into the European Union. This meant a *de facto* ban on all maize imports from the USA, since bulk shipments might contain some GM varieties not yet approved (*ibid.*).

Although regulatory authorities in the USA are opposed to mandatory labelling of GM products (see Chapter 9), the US farming community is heavily export-oriented and this has led to an informal movement encouraging labelling. In 1999 a prominent soy-processing and export firm in the USA announced that it would henceforth ask farmers to deliver their GM and non-GM soybeans in separate batches so that they could offer GM-free products to consumers in Europe and Japan. In the same year two large baby-food companies in the USA announced that they would soon switch to non-GM ingredients, not because of any evidence regarding lack of safety, but because they feared a Greenpeace-led boycott. The nation's major snack-food provider followed suit, announcing that it would no longer use GM corn (*ibid.*).

Is 'Fortress Europe' turning the anti-GM stance into a serious threat to global trade (against the USA) and world health (in developing countries)? Is the European Union using specious health concerns to protect their own farmers, who are heavily subsidised, from foreign competition?

The Cartagena Biosafety Protocol agreement

Here follows an attempt to give a simplified 'potted summary' of the Cartagena Biosafety Protocol agreement (Secretariat of the Convention on Biological Diversity, 2000). On 28 January 2000 representatives from over 130 governments met in Montreal to sign this agreement on transboundary transport of living GMOs. The agreement seeks to protect the environment of importing nations from the uncontrolled spread of live GMOs. On the basis of the precautionary principle, importing countries concerned about the safety of living GMOs have the right to block imports, even without conclusive scientific evidence that they will cause harm.

Shipments of commodities that may contain live GMOs must be clearly labelled. Products like food and feed derived from GMOs are excluded from the scope of the protocol, as are pharmaceuticals.

What are the implications for exporters of GMOs? Since the protocol covers organisms such as seeds, living fish and other living GMOs that are to be intentionally introduced into the environment, but excludes products derived from them, the direct impact should be minimal. However, it is not clear whether, for instance, the agreement includes a yoghurt containing GM bacteria. Also, it is not clear whether the restrictions apply to commercial releases only or to field trials as well. The protocol may have an impact on trade in raw materials and possibly on prices. The application of the precautionary principle could potentially lead to a non-scientific barrier to trade. On the other hand, since the protocol was agreed to by more than 130 countries, it could also lead to a general political and psychological legitimisation of gene technology and a calming down of the heated debate. Time will tell.

In summary ...

New regulatory systems are in place in South Africa and we hope that they will be robust enough to meet the needs of the country. Regulatory authorities in the USA are generally trusted. Due to trade pressures from Europe and Japan, however, the authorities are becoming more cautious. Europe uses the strong precautionary principle to regulate GMOs, and possibly to prevent imports of food and feed from the USA. The application of the Cartagena Bio-safety Protocol could result in a cooling down of this intensely heated debate.

Notes

[1] GMO Act 15/1997, Government Gazette No. 18029, Vol. 383, 23 May 1997, Pretoria.

[2] GMO Act Regulations, Government Gazette No. 6678, Vol. 413, 26 November 1999, Pretoria.

[3] 'New crops, new century, new challenges: how will scientists, farmers and consumers learn to love biotechnology, and what happens if they don't?' Speech by Dan Glickman to the National Press Club, 13 July 1999.

References and further reading

Birchard, K. (2000) European Commission to end *de facto* moratorium on GM products. *Lancet.* Vol. 356, p. 320.

Du Plessis, H. J., Brand, R. J., Glyn-Woods, C. and Goedhart, M. A. (1995) Genetic engineering leads to a herbicide-tolerant strawberry. *South African Journal of Science.* Vol. 91, p. 218.

Gaskell, G., Bauer, M. W., Durant, J. and Allum, N. C. (1999) Worlds apart? The reception of genetically modified foods in Europe and the US. *Science.* Vol. 285, pp. 384–387.

Hallerman, E. M. (2000) Administration announces sweeping assessment of federal agricultural and food biotech regulations. *ISB News Report.* June 2000, pp. 9–10.

Innovation Biotechnology (2000) Case study: The introduction of GM cotton into South Africa. In: *Biosafety 2: Advance research and procedures. Case studies for designated experts.* ICGEB Workshop, Florence, April 2000.

Paarlberg, R. (2000) The global food fight. *Foreign Affairs.* Vol. 79, pp. 24–38.

Secretariat of the Convention on Biological Diversity. (2000) *Cartagena Protocol on Biosafety to the Convention on Biological Diversity: Text and Annexes.* Secretariat of the Convention on Biological Diversity, Montreal.

Chapter 9

To label or not to label?

Background to the debate

There is a heated debate in many countries about whether or not to label foods that carry components derived from GM plants. In some cases this debate is clearly unnecessary. For example, if a soybean plant is modified genetically to resist infection of its roots by nematodes, and if that gene is active only in the roots, the beans themselves will be free of the foreign protein. Although the gene itself will be present in all the cells of the soybean plant, its protein product will be found in the roots only. In such a case there is no need to label the soybeans as genetically modified, as they will not contain the foreign protein. On the other hand, if the GM protein is present in the soybeans themselves, it may be necessary to label, as then the protein will be present in the food item. Therefore a critical issue is the sensitivity of the methods used to detect whether or not the gene or its product are present in the food item.

There are companies, such as Genetic ID in the USA, which claim they can detect minute amounts of tiny fragments (80 to 120 nucleotides) of transgenic DNA in virtually any foods (Fagan, 1999). They routinely and successfully analyse soups, pizza and other highly refined multi-ingredient products. In South Africa the Council for Scientific and Industrial Research (CSIR) has a system that can detect 0.1% of GM genes in food products.

Substantial equivalence and food labelling

I discussed the idea of substantial equivalence at some length in Chapter 6. Here we will look at the concept as it relates to the labelling of foods. Substantial equivalence is the starting point for assessing the safety of GM foods. The concept is used to identify similarities and differences between a GM food and a comparable traditional food.

The Paris-based Organisation for Economic Cooperation and Development (OECD) first applied the concept to food in 1986 (Anon). They were considering the safety of biotechnology products and reached a consensus that, while recombinant DNA techniques may produce plants that express a combination of traits that are not observed in nature, such changes will often be more predictable than those resulting from traditional breeding. This is because the techniques involved are more precise. They concluded that any health risks associated with GM plants should be assessed in the same way as those associated with non-GM plants. They also noted that the foods derived from GM plants should be as safe as those from conventional plants.

Others agreed with this stance and in 1989 a report of the United States National Research Council, published by the National Academy Press, observed that organisms modified by molecular methods enable us to predict phenotypic expression much more accurately. Similarly an editorial in the journal *Nature* in 1992 (Anon., p. 2) stated that 'the same physical and biological laws govern the response of organisms [such as plants] modified by modern ... methods and those produced by classical methods'. This last quotation is remarkable as it expresses the widely held scientific consensus that our ability to predict food safety is superior for genetically engineered foods.

The OECD returned to the question of food safety in a report published in 1993. 'Modern biotechnology broadens the scope of the genetic changes that can be made in food organisms, and broadens the scope of possible sources of foods. This does not inherently lead to foods that are less safe than those developed by conventional techniques. Therefore, evaluation of foods and food components obtained from organisms developed by the application of the newer techniques does not necessitate a fundamental change in established principles, nor does it require a different standard of safety' (Anon., 1993). Again in 1998 the OECD stated, 'While establishment of substantial equivalence is not a safety evaluation *per se*, when substantial equivalence is established between a new food and the conventional ... antecedent, it establishes the safety of the new food relative to an existing food and no further safety consideration is needed' (Anon., 1998).

The concept of substantial equivalence in new foods is not, as asserted by Millstone *et al.* (1999), a scientific principle. It is merely a kind of regulatory shorthand for defining those new foods that do not raise safety issues that

144

require special, intensive, case-by-case scrutiny (Miller, 1999). The FAO/WHO expert consultation on safety aspects of GM foods of plant origin (FAO/WHO, 2000) concluded that the concept of substantial equivalence provided the best assurance of safety of GM foods.

Safety testing and GM foods

We considered food safety testing in Chapter 6, but I will mention a few issues pertinent to food labelling here. What does the FDA take into account when testing the safety of new foods? They consider whether the food contains:

■ a substance completely new to the food supply;
■ an allergen (e.g. a peanut protein in a potato); or
■ increased levels of toxins normally found in food.

An example of the latter is the level of the compound solanine found in potatoes. Some new potato varieties, developed by conventional breeding methods, contain harmful levels of this naturally occurring toxin.

Millstone *et al.* (1999) demand extensive, complicated and hugely expensive biological, toxicological and immunological testing of foods from GM plants. In essence they treat these foods like pharmaceuticals. They appear to ignore the fact that many products on the market are derived from 'wide crosses' between different species or even different genera of plants. These hybridisation experiments are far less precise than modern biotechnology but the products enter the marketplace each year without pre-market review or special labelling. Examples that spring to mind are the peach mutant called a nectarine and the tangelo, a hybrid between a tangerine and a grapefruit.

In December 1997, the United Kingdom's Advisory Committee on Novel Foods and Processes (ACNFP) announced a change in their policy on substantial equivalence. Previously, the ACNFP had considered a food product derived from a GM crop to be substantially equivalent to the non-GM product based on the following criteria:

■ gross composition;
■ properties, such as texture and moisture content;
■ nutritional content;

- the type of processing (industrial or domestic) that the food might undergo;
- toxin and allergen content;
- likely consumption patterns.

In 1997 they added the requirement that the food should not contain any GM DNA or protein. This stipulation excludes refined foods derived from GM crops, such as hot pressed oil, white sugar and starch. These foods are considered to be substantially equivalent to their conventional counterparts on the grounds that food-processing techniques destroy both DNA and protein. All other ingredients derived from GM crops, such as flour and protein extracts, require full safety evaluations via chemical analyses to determine whether they contain novel DNA and/or protein, in either intact or degraded form. Manufacturers are required to provide data to substantiate this. If the food product contains GM DNA or protein, it will need to go through the full regulatory process; if none is detected a notification process will suffice.

How can we test for GM-free food products?

Although a number of methods are available to test whether food products are GM-free, there are no official standards outlining what constitutes a GM food or what makes a particular food product GM-free. Some tests are based on DNA analysis and others determine the presence of the gene product, the protein. They range from a three- to five-minute in-the-field test to very involved laboratory investigations. The quickest and easiest method is a dipstick test, for example 'TraitCheck' which comes in a kit costing about $6 per test. However, this is a qualitative test and does not satisfy labelling rules that require less than a given percentage of GM material in a product. Quantitative protein tests cost about $25 per test. DNA tests are even more expensive, at around $250 per sample.

These methods continue to become more sensitive. The most important question is at what level the presence of DNA and/or protein is meaningful. Finally, we will never be able to show that food products are GM-free because we would need to test these foods for every possible GM product. As assessment methods become more sensitive, we will have to continuously re-evaluate these food products. We need to establish a definition or a standard that determines when a food product is GM-free.

Separating GM and non-GM products

Let us take an example of a particular product that contains detectable levels of a novel DNA or protein. Let us further disregard the question of whether that DNA or protein could possibly be harmful. Let us simply consider the case of a manufacturer who wishes to produce a food product that is free of the novel DNA or protein. How easy is it to separate GM crops from non-GM crops?

The most efficient way to transport and market crops such as soybeans is to combine the produce from thousands of farms. To keep herbicide-resistant soybeans separate from non-GM soybeans, for example, will necessitate keeping produce from some fields or farms separate, resulting in a major increase in transport costs all along the chain. In any case, cross-pollination and the mixing of crops through the handling and distribution network make complete separation of GM and conventional crops impossible in practice.

Some specialty soybeans, accounting for approximately 1% of the US crop, are grown under contract under particular conditions and are kept separate at harvest time. They are shipped in special containers to supply, for example, the Japanese tofu market. The contract specifies particular purity tolerances and consumers pay a significant premium above the commodity price. These soybeans are three times more expensive than ordinary ones.

In the case of maize, in 1998 the USA exported $200 million-worth to Europe. Although this represents only about 1% of the entire crop, American farmers would not like to see this export avenue closed. In 1999 Europe banned the import of GM crops and the door was indeed firmly shut. This would not present too much of a problem were separating GM from non-GM crops a simple matter. But America's grain-handling system is designed for bulk, not discrimination. The same applies to the export of soybeans. According to the American Soybean Association (*The Economist*, 19 June 1999) there are ten points on the trip from farm to ship at which exporters deliberately mix different types of soybeans to improve their quality. Trying to set up systems to separate the vast quantities of maize and soybeans that flow through America would roughly double the final price of non-GM foods. For food manufacturers such as Unilever this would mean a 25% premium on the final cost of goods.

It is not clear who would be willing to pay such inflated prices. In the case of organic produce, consumers are willing to spend more, but the current backlash against GM foods indicates that consumers would not be willing to pay more for these foods. In any case, genetic modification is supposed to lower food prices, not raise them! The upshot may be that, in the short term, the dealers will have to bear the costs of keeping GM and non-GM foods separate, in order to achieve gains in the long term by winning consumers around to the idea that the new GM foods are actually a good buy.

The question that still remains is how free is GM-free food? Protein Technologies International, part of DuPont, has set up a distinct processing system in order to sell GM-free lecithin. They guarantee that it will be 99.5% GM-free, as some contamination appears to be unavoidable. Is 99.5% sufficiently GM-free? Food manufacturers who are promising consumers GM-free products must be told what this means. Furthermore, are the scientific tests actually sensitive enough to detect 0.5% of a foreign gene or protein in a given product? All these ambiguities are proving to be extremely frustrating to traders and trade officials.

The question of labelling

The pros and cons of labelling

Let us now consider the pros and cons of labelling GM products. The European Union has made labelling mandatory while the USA appears to be moving towards voluntary labelling. In South Africa and elsewhere on the African continent the debate continues.

Requiring producers of manufactured foods to disclose key information about the nutritional characteristics of foods has made consumers more selective about what they buy. Although rising rates of obesity in the USA make one wonder about the effectiveness of such labelling in that country, labelling foods is unquestionably a good health-based policy. We cannot say the same about labelling products simply because they are derived from GM crops, because such labelling does not necessarily provide any health-related information. In the case of a GM tomato with a significantly higher vitamin C content, however, labelling could provide consumers with useful health-related information. These products would need to be labelled according to both the American and European systems. If there is any meaningful difference in nutrition or safety, the food must be labelled. But the mere fact that a product has, at some stage in its development, been derived from a GM plant does not have any health implications. There is a danger, however, that the consumer will interpret mandatory labels on GM foods as health warnings.

Karil Kochenderfer, Director of International Trade and Environmental Affairs of the organisation Grocery Manufacturers of America has stated that 'The reality is that ... a label indicating genetic modification mistakenly raises questions about the safety of biotech foods that have been reviewed and found safe by regulatory agencies worldwide. Even proponents of biotech labelling, such as the Center for Science in the Public Interest, acknowledge that a congressional mandatory labelling proposal won't work, because such a label "would become a scare label"' (http://agbioworld.org, 27 April 2000).

We also need to consider what kinds of products should be labelled. Let us take the hypothetical example of a tomato modified with a bean gene and a bean modified with a tomato gene. It would be straightforward to label the vegetables themselves but on what grounds would we label vegetable soup containing both these GMOs? Before processing, we would be able to identify each vegetable as a GM product. In the soup, however, the genes and proteins of both tomatoes and beans would be blended together. If we labelled the soup, we would be doing so based solely on the method of crop breeding and not on the composition of the final product.

With reference to the examples above, labelling, especially in these early days of public acceptance of GM foods, may be a good idea. However, we must then make labelling for all production methods mandatory, including halal, kosher and organic. Consumers have a right to know that they are, for example, drinking organically prepared apple juice or cider that may well contain life-threatening levels of the bacterium *Escherichia coli* (Dingman, 2000), or that they are eating organically grown maize that might contain dangerous fungal toxins. But why stop there? How about

CHAPTER 9: TO LABEL OR NOT TO LABEL

dictating that farmers log volumes and types of pesticides applied to crops? And should we not label beef to inform consumers about how the cow was raised and on what it was fed? Such a list would become absurd and the costs would be enormous. But this is the logical outcome of a labelling policy based not on food content but on method of production. It is based not on the consumers' 'need to know' but on their 'right to know'. If we advocate the latter then we should provide information across the board and bear the financial burden as consumers.

Mandatory labelling

What has been the effect of the European Union's legislation on mandatory labelling introduced in 1999? In an article entitled 'Genetically modified label confuses UK shoppers', journalist Steve Stecklow reports that Britain's Minister for Agriculture called mandatory labelling 'a triumph for consumer rights to better information' (*The Wall Street Journal*, 27 October 1999; on-line version).

Britain went on to enact the toughest labelling standards in Europe, requiring even restaurants, caterers and bakers to list GM ingredients. Violations were punishable by fines. As J. R. Bell, head of the government department dealing with additives and novel foods put it, 'This is not a health issue in any way. This is a question of choice, of consumer choice' (*ibid.*). But in fact, as a direct result of the labelling law, there is hardly any choice now at all. Consumers have become locked into the idea that GM foods are bad. In their eyes, the label condemns a food product despite the fact that regulatory agencies consider it to be as safe as its non-GM counterpart.

One example of the impact of GM labelling on sales is that of tomato puree made from GM tomatoes with improved pulping qualities. The British supermarket chain, J. Sainsbury PLC, introduced the GM-labelled puree in 1996. It was cheaper than other brands and outsold them by 30%. However, as the GM controversy heated up, sales slowed down. By the end of 1999, according to Sainsbury's environmental manager, sales 'absolutely fell through the floor' (*ibid.*).

Another example of the labelling dilemma is the case of cheese produced using an enzyme produced by GM bacteria. Traditionally, an enzyme called rennet, extracted from the lining of calves' stomachs, is used to make cheese set. To appease vegetarians, many European cheese makers have switched to an enzyme called chymosin that is produced by GM bacteria. There is no evidence that any GM substance remains in cheese after production. Nevertheless, the use of chymosin remains a target.

Ironically, Greenpeace have stated that they do not oppose the use of pharmaceuticals produced by genetic engineering. Since 1985 nearly one hundred different biotechnology drugs have been approved for use. Enthusiasm continues to grow for the promise of gene therapy to combat diseases such as HIV/AIDS, cancer and diabetes. It is difficult to explain the difference between dosing a diabetic with insulin derived from GM bacteria and eating cheese produced using a product derived from a GM bacterium.

Labelling: the international situation

It is probably risky to include in this book an analysis of where various countries stand on the issue of labelling of GM foods. It is likely that, by the time this book is published, this section will be out of date. However, for the record, here is the situation at the time of going to press:

- In August 1999 Japan decided that, as of April 2001, foods derived from GM crops must be labelled. Many food products are exempt on the grounds that DNA or protein resulting from gene alteration cannot be detected. Labelling is required in cases where GM material is one of the top three ingredients by mass and where it accounts for at least 5% of the total mass. This is less stringent than the European Union rule that requires warning labels when at least one ingredient contains more than 1% GM material.

- South Korea's parliament enacted a law in July 1999 to regulate GM food labelling. The government has yet to decide which products should be labelled.

- The governments of Australia and New Zealand decided in August 1999 to order mandatory labelling of all GM foods. The law is expected to be enacted during 2001.

- Malaysia is typical of most Southeast Asian nations in that it has no laws requiring labelling of GM foods.

- Thailand also has no labelling laws at present but is concerned about its food exports to Europe. In 1999 the Greek customs authorities seized a container of Thai canned tuna, demanding proof that the consignment did not contain GMOs. This highlighted the potential threat to Thai exports and the need for proper labelling.

■ China remains silent on the labelling issue. Like many African countries, China is far more interested in boosting agricultural productivity through GM crops than introducing strict labelling laws.

Who should bear the costs of labelling?

Should consumers have the right to know whether they are consuming GM foods? Yes, indeed they should, as long as they are prepared to bear the costs. These costs include, among other things, the need for farmers to segregate crops; dedicated grain storage silos to keep GM deliveries separate from their non-GM counterparts; and food inspectors to test shipments.

We therefore need to ask whether the majority of consumers, who understand that there is no health difference between GM and non-GM foods, should pay this cost. Markets should dictate whether or not consumers will choose low food prices or labelling. After all, if you were to ask a hundred people if they would want to know whether there was GM material in their food, most would say yes. If you then asked the same hundred people the same question, but added that finding out would cost them, say, five cents extra per loaf of bread, far fewer would be interested.

In summary ...

Some countries, such as the United Kingdom, mandate labelling of food as being GM-free, although the meaningfulness of such labels is debatable. Others, such as the USA, favour voluntary labelling. Perhaps in countries where consumers are opposed to GM crops and foods, labelling will be necessary. But consumers in those countries will have to bear the extra costs involved.

References

Anon. (1986) *Recombinant DNA Safety Considerations.* OECD, Paris.

Anon. (1992) *Nature.* Vol. 356, pp. 1–2.

Anon. (1993) *Safety Evaluation of Foods Derived by Modern Biotechnology.* OECD, Paris.

Anon. (1998) *Report of the OECD Workshop on the Toxicological and Nutritional Testing of Novel Foods.* SG/ICGB(98)1, September 1998. OECD, Paris.

Dingman, D. W. (2000) Growth of *Escherichia coli* O157:H7 in bruised apple (*Malus domestica*) tissue as influenced by cultivar, date of harvest, and source. *Applied and Environmental Microbiology.* Vol. 66, pp. 1077–1083.

Fagan, J. (1999) GM food labeling. *Nature Biotechnology.* Vol. 17, p. 836.

FAO/WHO. (2000) Safety aspects of genetically modified foods of plant origin. Report of a Joint FAO/WHO Expert Consultation on foods derived from biotechnology, 29 May–2 June 2000.

Miller, H. J. (1999) Substantial equivalence: its uses and abuses. *Nature Biotechnology.* Vol. 17, pp. 1042–1043.

Millstone, E., Brunner, E. and Mayer, S. (1999) Beyond 'substantial equivalence'. *Nature.* Vol. 401, pp. 525–526.

Chapter 10

What's in it for Africa?

The 'Doubly Green Revolution'

Gordon Conway is President of the Rockefeller Foundation. In his book *The Doubly Green Revolution* (1997) he states that more than three-quarters of a billion people are living in a world where food is plentiful, and yet they are denied it. If we were to add up the world's food production and then divide it equally among the world's population, each man, woman and child would receive a daily average of over 2 700 calories of energy. This is enough to prevent hunger and is probably sufficient to allow everyone to lead a healthy life.

The reality, however, is harshly different. While Europeans and North Americans enjoy an average of 3 500 calories per day, people living in sub-Saharan Africa eke out an existence on far less. Tim Dyson (1999) has calculated the food shortage that sub-Saharan Africa could experience by the year 2025. He bases this on the average cereal yield during the period 1989–1991 of 1.165 tons per hectare. He projects an average yield of 1.536 tons per hectare in the year 2025. If that is the case, sub-Saharan Africa will experience a grain shortfall of 88.7 million tons in 2025. Compare that with, for example, the Middle East, which had an average yield during the same period of 1.642 tons per hectare. Dyson projects a yield of 2.468 tons per hectare in 2025, representing a grain shortfall of 132.7 million tons. The huge difference between these two scenarios is that the Middle East can afford to buy in food supplies, while sub-Saharan Africa cannot. What, then, is the solution? In Conway's eyes it will require a 'Doubly Green Revolution'.

What does Gordon Conway mean by the term 'Doubly Green Revolution'? The Green Revolution, which started in the 1940s in Mexico, aimed to improve the yields of basic food crops such as maize and wheat. Using genetic breeding techniques, scientists bred high-yielding lines using indigenous plant varieties suited to Mexican conditions. Success came very quickly. In 1948 farmers planted 1 400 tons of improved maize seed and for the first time since 1910 Mexico did not need to import maize. By the 1960s maize yields were averaging over 1 000 kilograms per hectare. Total production had increased from two to six million tons. Improved breeding programmes spread to South America, India, Asia and Africa, resulting in similar yield increases in wheat, rice and other crops. By the 1980s new Green Revolution varieties dominated half of sub-Saharan Africa's maize and wheat crop.

However, all was not well. Yield improvement was not solely attributable to the new varieties. They were necessary but not sufficient for success. Their potential could only be realised if the crops were supplemented with fertilisers and optimal supplies of water. Both of these are in short supply for most African farmers and Conway admits that the Green Revolution has been least successful in sub-Saharan Africa. Cereal yields have changed little over the past 40 years and cereal production per capita has steadily declined. Most of the yield gains in maize occurred in the 1950s and early 1960s. Since then yield increases have been very erratic.

So much for the Green Revolution. What about the Doubly Green Revolution? Gordon Conway argues that the only way to improve crop production in the twenty-first century is to combine conservation of the environment with productivity. He calls for scientists and farmers to forge genuine partnerships in an effort to design better crops. He also urges them to develop and rediscover alternatives to inorganic fertilisers and pesticides, to improve soil and water management, and to enhance earning opportunities for the poor, especially women.

To quote Conway (pp. 151–152), 'Genetic engineering has a special value for agricultural production in developing countries. It has the potential ...[of] creating new plant varieties ... that not only deliver higher yields but contain the internal solutions to biotic and abiotic challenges, reducing the need for chemical inputs such as fungicides and pesticides, and increasing tolerance to drought, salinity, chemical toxicity and other adverse circumstances. Most important, genetic engineering is likely to be as valuable a tool for the lower-potential lands as for those with high potential. It can be aimed not only at increasing productivity but also at achieving higher levels of stability and sustainability.'

Agriculture in Africa

Food production challenges

One of the greatest challenges today for sub-Saharan Africa is to improve the nutrient status of agricultural lands. Some soils are naturally richer in nutrients than others and can be exploited for a while. Eventually, however, they lose nutrients that have to be replaced. Without nutrient replacement there is no agricultural sustainability. African farmers cannot, on the whole, afford synthetic nutrients. They have to rely instead on growing more organic matter in the soil and ploughing this in to return nutrients to the soil. Productivity is often low, which reduces the amount of organic material available to be returned to the soil after harvesting. It is therefore imperative to increase the amount of organic matter grown in African soil.

In Africa, crop production per unit of land cultivated is the lowest in the agricultural world. Florence Wambugu is Director of the International Service for the Acquisition of Agri-Biotech Applications' (ISAAA) AfriCenter in Nairobi, Kenya. She cites the example of sweet potato, a staple crop, which yields six tons per hectare in Africa, compared to the global average of 14 tons per hectare. China produces on average 18 tons per hectare, three times the African average. African production could potentially double if viral diseases could be controlled using transgenic technology. Wambugu goes on to say that Africa imports at least 25% of its grain. The use of biotechnology to increase local grain production is far preferable to this expensive dependency (Wambugu, 1999).

During the twentieth century the world population increased from about 1.5 to six billion people. Symbolically, we reached the six billion mark on 12 October 1999. Remarkably enough, we produce enough food on a global scale today to meet the basic requirements of every person on earth. This achievement is largely the result of the successful implementation of several technologies that form the basis of modern agriculture. These include mechanisation, the production of protective chemicals and fertilisers, and improved crop breeding.

Despite our capacity to produce the volumes of food required, however, food production is not uniform throughout the world and transportation is clearly inadequate. We must address these problems and it would be foolish to rule out the use of GM crops, especially those that are resistant to diseases and can tolerate drier conditions. Of course, the use of GM crops is not the only answer to our current and future food shortages. Improved farming techniques, better transportation and infrastructure, and less corruption in food distribution can all contribute to solving this problem.

Examples from Africa

Anatole Krattiger (1998), the former Executive Director of ISAAA, gives the following real-life example of agricultural problems in Africa. In an address to a biotechnology conference in 1998, he told of a man from the highlands of Mount Kenya who used to have a seven-acre farm. His three sons each inherited one quarter of the farm while he retained the remaining quarter. On this land they had to produce enough to nourish their families, as well as a surplus to enable them to barter with neighbours and to earn money to educate and clothe their children. Now there are many more children, parents and grandparents to feed from the same seven acres. After they are fed what surpluses can be produced? Their only options are either to sink further into poverty or to encroach on marginal lands.

Agriculture is the engine of growth in Africa and most of the developing world, where nearly 90% of people live. Almost half of Africa's 600 million people survive on less than $0.65 per day (World Bank, 2000). This poses a challenging start to the millennium, but we do not have to continue in this way. Nigeria's President Olesugun Obasanjo, himself a farmer, states the following, 'As long as farming remains, at best, marginally rewarding, young men and women will drift away from the rural areas to increase the battalions of the urban poor. The idea, therefore, that African agriculture should be based only on a half-hectare holding is, to say the least, unappetizing. I want to see people encouraged. I want to see the evolution of young, emergent, commercial farmers who will be holding, not a half-hectare of land, but five to 10 to 20 hectares of land, and for whom the city will have no big attraction.'[1]

All is not doom and gloom for African agriculture. In a speech in Malawi in March 2000 Norman Borlaug, winner of the Nobel Peace Prize and father of the Green Revolution, indicated that food production per capita in some sub-Saharan African countries increased slightly faster than the population during the 1990s. However, this was not uniformly the case,

CHAPTER 10: WHAT'S IN IT FOR AFRICA?

especially in countries like Ethiopia and Sudan, which have been ravaged by both drought and war (see Table 5).

Country	1997	1998	1999
Benin	120	119	133
Burkina Faso	101	109	106
Eritrea	87	115	110
Ethiopia	104	97	98
Ghana	112	114	128
Guinea	108	113	112
Malawi	93	104	115
Mozambique	101	106	104
Nigeria	116	122	126
Sudan	136	133	128
Tanzania	79	82	80
Uganda	87	91	93
Zambia	82	78	83

(Source: FAO AGROSTAT, October 1999)

TABLE 5: Index of *per capita* food production in sub-Saharan Africa[a].

[a] Relative values compared with an arbitrary level of 100 in 1989–1991.

Technology and productivity

Dr Borlaug went on to say that the new tools of genetic engineering will allow us to speed up the development of much more nutritional food crop varieties that are more tolerant of drought, heat, cold and soil mineral toxicity, and more resistant to insect pests and diseases. In his Noble Peace Prize acceptance speech in 1970, Borlaug said that the Green Revolution had won a temporary success in our war against hunger. If fully imple-mented, it could provide sufficient food for humankind through the end of the twentieth century. But he warned that, unless the fright-ening spectre of human population growth was curbed, the success of the Green Revolution would be ephemeral. In a more recent speech, Borlaug stated that we need sophisticated scientific technology to boost agricultural production. Citing the examples of China and Brazil, which have more than doubled their production of cereals through genetic engineering, he said that biotechnology was the surest way of ensuring food security in Africa and other developing countries (8 June 2000; http://www.agbioworld.org).

A pertinent question is whether farmers will be permitted to use this new technology. Access to this technology will be the salvation of the poor. It will not help, as some would have us believe, to keep them wedded to out-dated, low-yielding and more costly production technology.

Let us also not forget that poverty destroys the environment. Hence, anything we do to alleviate poverty serves the environment and human health. The Green Revolution has done much to improve agricultural productivity, but for the poor to take advantage of this they need access not only to seed but also to fertilisers and irrigation. GM crops could reduce dependence on both these requirements, so that farmers would need to purchase seeds only.

Critics of biotechnology who claim that Africa has no chance of benefiting from GM technology often state that small-scale farmers will be 'forced' to buy GM seeds. However, farmers in Africa have benefited for years from using hybrid seed obtained from local and multinational companies. Transgenic seeds are simply a further improvement on these hybrids.

It is interesting to note that very few of the critics are the small-scale farmers themselves. Rather, they are armchair experts imposing a 'victim mentality' on people who could potentially benefit from access to GM seed. If we ask Africans for their opinions on the advantages of GM crops for sustainable agriculture, the responses are overwhelmingly positive. While improved farming practices can go part of the way to enhancing productivity, GM crops resistant to diseases and pests, and able to grow in marginal land due to increased drought tolerance, can play an enormous role.

Problems facing African agriculture

Let us consider some agricultural problems that are specific to Africa. According to Professor Mark Laing, a plant pathologist from KwaZulu-Natal in South Africa, the two most important traits for African crops are the ability to withstand soil acidity and drought stress. He refers to a study on commercial vegetable production carried out in that province, which showed that soil acidity and drought stress accounted for over 80% of yield losses.

Diseases and pests accounted for the remaining 20% (Askew, 1995). A similar picture emerges from a study of community gardens: water stress, soil acidity and low phosphate and potassium levels were the dominant yield-reducing factors (Adey *et al.*, 1998).

Soil acidity and nutrients

In most of Africa virgin soils vary from acid to very acid, with pH values of between 3.5 and 4.5. Cabbage production, for instance, requires the application of about 18 tons of lime per hectare. Acidity in the soil causes aluminium and manganese to become soluble and this leads to toxicity. On the other hand, critical minerals such as molybdenum precipitate, and are therefore unavailable to plants.

In Africa, levels of phosphate in the soil are often low. For instance, whereas phosphate concentrations in the soil may be in the order of two parts per million (ppm), cabbage requires levels of between 60 and 80 ppm and maize requires 40 ppm. Sources of phosphate are limited and expensive. Organic sources such as compost are usually too low in phosphate to be useful. Gardeners in South Africa know all too well how important and costly it is to apply compounds like Super-phosphate.

Drought stress

Africa experiences frequent droughts and plants are often exposed to heat stress. Therefore GM crop research in Africa, and especially in South Africa, needs to focus on developing crops that can tolerate heat stress and drought, while being able to grow in acidic soils that are low in phosphates.

Africa is home to a large number of indigenous plants with a remarkable ability to withstand desiccation. These so-called 'resurrection plants' are found in deserts and grow in cracks in rocks. Scientists at the University of Cape Town are using one of these resurrection plants, the monocot *Xerophyta viscosa*, as a source of genes to develop drought-tolerant crops.

In addition, many of the traits listed in Table 3 (see page 60) that are currently under development will be of immense value to Africa. Some of these include:

160

- salinity tolerance;
- enhanced phosphorous and nitrogen uptake;
- resistance to the parasitic weed *Striga*;
- resistance to viruses and bacteria;
- delayed ripening of fruit and vegetables;
- improved amino acid content of forage crops.

African crops and diseases

Let us now look as some crops and diseases that are specific to Africa:

Cassava

Known to western societies as a source of tapioca, cassava is a staple food in much of Africa. The leaves and starchy roots of this plant, when powdered, boiled, fried or fermented, make up the world's third-largest source of calories, after rice and maize. Plant breeders working in East Africa have succeeded in increasing the size and number of edible roots. Yields improved at first, but over the years these have reached a plateau due to increasing losses as a result of fungal, viral and bacterial diseases. In some years, cassava mosaic virus has almost wiped out the entire cassava crop in some African countries. Although the introduction of foreign genes into cassava is not yet routine, scientists have produced virus-resistant varieties (C. Fauquet, personal communication, 2001).

Another problem with cassava is that it contains high levels of cyanide. Preparation involves three to five days of labour-intensive treatment, soaking the cassava in water and scrubbing it to remove the cyanide. Cyanide levels could be reduced by genetic engineering.

Bananas

In the western world, bananas and their close relatives, plantains, are a snack and a dessert. But in western and central Africa they provide more than one-quarter of all food calories. The United Nations Food and Agriculture Organisation (FAO) ranks bananas as the world's fourth most important food crop. Although banana transformation is not easy, workers in Belgium have succeeded in introducing genes encoding resistance to the most serious fungal disease.

Sweet potatoes

Many people in eastern and southern Africa eat sweet potatoes as a subsistence crop. Scientists from the USA, South Africa, Kenya and Uganda have succeeded in improving the protein content of sweet potatoes by a factor of four, from the traditional 3% to 12%. This could have a significant effect on the lives of many people in Africa (Qaim, 1999).

The ISAAA has identified sweet potatoes in Kenya as an 'orphan' crop. This is a crop that has minor international appeal but that is important to semi-subsistence farmers in developing countries. Sweet potatoes, which are mainly grown by resource-poor women in Africa, are important for food security as they yield more food energy and micronutrients per unit area than any other crop (ISAAA, 1999).

Despite the crop being fairly robust, pests and diseases, notably viruses and weevils, cause significant yield losses. In a joint project, Monsanto, the Kenya Agricultural Research Institute (KARI), ISAAA and the International Potato Centre are addressing these problems using genetic engineering. Monsanto has signed a royalty-free licensing agreement that allows KARI to use their proprietary technology and to share it with other African countries in the future. Kenyan farmers could receive transgenic virus-resistant sweet potatoes by 2002 and weevil-resistant varieties by 2004.

Maize

Maize streak virus is an endemic virus that causes havoc in maize crops in Africa. Figure 24 (see page 124 in the colour section) shows the effect of the virus on a plant and the crop in a field.

Maize streak virus is unusual in that its genetic material is DNA instead of RNA, the genetic material found in most plant viruses. For technical reasons, coat protein-mediated resistance (see Chapter 3) is unlikely to work for this virus. Scientists in South Africa and the United Kingdom are working on alternative ways of developing resistance to this devastating disease that affects a crop that some people on the African continent eat three times a day.

Striga

Striga is not a crop, but a parasitic weed that is a pest in Africa. It is a particular scourge because, by a quirk of nature, it gravitates towards weak

162

maize, rice and sorghum plants on poorly managed farms. The Rockefeller Foundation is paying particular attention to *Striga* because the problem could be overcome if local farmers treated crop seed with a modern herbicide. According to Gary Toenniessen of the Foundation (Anon., 1999, p. 341), such treatment would involve applying a minuscule amount of herbicide, in fact as little as five grams per hectare planted. This treatment will only be effective, however, if the crops themselves are genetically modified to tolerate the herbicide (see Chapter 3).

A report produced by Andrea Johanson and Catherine Ives entitled *An inventory of agricultural biotechnology for the eastern and central African region* (http://www.iia.msu.edu/absp) makes very interesting reading. Indeed there is a considerable amount of work being done around the world that could specifically benefit these regions.

GMOs in Africa

Edible vaccines

One of the most exciting applications of GM crops for Africa is the prospect of edible **vaccines**. Instead of being vaccinated with a needle, vaccines will be delivered in the form of an edible fruit or vegetable. The gene, coding for the vaccine, will be introduced into the fruit or vegetable, which will then produce the vaccine product. Those of us who remember the polio epidemics of the 1950s will recall lining up at school to have a sugar cube impregnated with the vaccine placed on our tongue. This and other polio vaccines have resulted in the very real prospect of poliomyelitis being completely eradicated from the human population by 2005. Imagine in the near future, hundreds of rural children throughout Africa lining up at school for a banana that could immunise them against life-threatening diseases such as dysentery and diarrhoea.

One of the reasons why smallpox could be eradicated worldwide was because medical practitioners could reuse needles. This was in the days before the onset of HIV/AIDS. The two greatest expenses in modern vaccination programmes are needles and cold storage of the vaccine; edible vaccines would solve both problems. The World Health Organisation estimates that over 12 million children under the age of five die each year from infectious diseases (http://www.who.int). Vaccines already on the market could save at least two million children per year.

Scientists at several universities and research institutes are conducting trials in which they feed mice foods such as potatoes, tomatoes or alfalfa sprouts that have been genetically altered to produce antigens. These **antigens** elicit an immune response to diseases such as hepatitis B, cholera and travellers' diarrhoea. Immune system 'effector sites' recognise these antigens. These sites are part of the mucosa-associated lymphoid tissue, or MALT, which lines the digestive tract. In the USA, human clinical trials have been in progress for a number of years to test the effects of a plant-based vaccine on a toxin produced by *Escherichia coli*. Results have been extremely promising.

An added advantage to edible vaccines is that only part of the virus is used in the immunisation. Again readers who remember the polio epidemics of the 1950s may recall the debate about the relative merits of two different types of vaccine. One vaccine, developed by Jonas Salk in 1955, administered killed virus. The other, developed later by Albert Sabin, used an attenuated form of the live virus. In the latter case the poliovirus was grown for a number of generations through a primate host and this rendered it non-virulent to humans. Both vaccines held potential dangers. It was possible that the Salk vaccine might have contained a few live viruses that had escaped being killed. In the case of Sabin's vaccine it was possible that a particular batch could have remained pathogenic to humans. In the end, Sabin's vaccine proved more effective than Salk's. Genetic engineering has now enabled scientists to produce 'sub-unit' vaccines that use only a part of the virus to generate immunity. Indeed the sub-unit vaccine may be as small as a single viral protein and thus much safer than either of the earlier vaccines.

Orally administered vaccines are most appropriate for protection against pathogens that enter via mucosal surfaces such as the digestive tract, respiratory system or urogenital tracts. At the University of Cape Town in South Africa, scientists are developing oral and other vaccines that act against human papilloma virus, one of the agents causing cervical cancer.

This is the main cause of cancer fatalities among women in the developing world. A similar programme is being developed to try to produce edible vaccines against HIV/AIDS. The aim of these research programmes is to produce vaccines for African diseases that cost cents rather than dollars. This research is still in the developmental stages and a great deal of work is needed to ensure effectiveness, safety and practicality. (See also Chapter 11.)

Antigen: a foreign substance that induces an immune response in the body, notably the production of antibodies. (An antibody is a class of blood proteins produced in response to antigens that counteracts these antigens.)

Escherichia coli: a normal member of the human gut bacterial flora that is usually not harmful. However, certain strains, which produce a toxin, can result in diarrhoea and even death.

Vaccine: a preparation used to stimulate the body's production of antibodies in order to produce immunity to a disease.

The GMO debate in North America and Europe

How should people in Africa respond to the current outcry in Europe against GM crops and foods? And how should they reconcile this with the relatively greater acceptance of the technology in the USA and Canada? In order to understand these contrasting attitudes it would be helpful to go back in time to the 1970s when GMOs first hit the headlines.

In those days, most of the debate took place in the USA. Scientists imposed a moratorium on genetic engineering until rules, codes of conduct, and guidelines for experiments could be laid down. That, however, did not stop the American public from engaging in a very energetic public debate, somewhat along the lines of what Europe is experiencing today. Slowly the American public began to see the benefits of the new technology. The most tangible evidence of this was the appearance on Wall Street of listed biotechnology companies. Although most of these small start-up companies have long since been bought out by major pharmaceutical and chemical companies, the fact is that biotechnology and GMOs are 'old hat' to many Americans. They have been around for long enough, without causing any harm to humans, animals or the environment, to have been generally accepted in the USA and Canada.

Although there are numerous biotechnology companies in Europe, the GMO debate in the 1970s was less intense than in the USA. Thus, public awareness of GMOs does not have as long a history in Europe. In addition, scientists and politicians in Europe, and particularly in the United Kingdom, have badly mishandled public health issues like the debacle around 'Mad Cow Disease' (bovine spongiform encephalitis or BSE). Not surprisingly, Europeans have emerged from this scare with very little trust in scientists wishing to assure them of the safety of anything!

Furthermore, Europe has enough food, so why should Europeans want to approve of GM crops or the sale of GM foods? As discussed in Chapter 3, first generation GM crops largely benefit seed companies and producers, who may or may not pass on savings to the consumer. It is only when second generation GM foods hit the supermarkets (see Chapter 4) that the consumer feels the benefits. Europe is unlikely to soften its position until that occurs. In addition, European countries subsidise their farmers. It is certainly not in their interests to import food from America. Banning the importation of GM crops and foods is thus an ideal way of limiting such imports.

Africa and the anti-GMO lobby

How, then, should Africa respond to these American and European agendas? Firstly, we do not have enough food to feed our populations and agricultural productivity is far less than in the northern hemisphere. Secondly, Africa is a continent particularly dependent on agriculture and the distinction between consumers and farmers is often blurred. Let us remember that a person with enough food has many problems; a person without enough food has only one.

Although African scientists like Florence Wambugu (1999) applaud the use of biotechnology to improve crop and food production in Africa, some journalists disagree. Declan Walsh wrote an article in Nairobi for *The Independent* in the United Kingdom, entitled, 'America finds ready market for GM food – the hungry'.[2] A ghastly photograph accompanies the article. It depicts a man dying from starvation lying next to food sacks. The caption reads, 'A Sudanese man collapsing as he waits for food from the UN World Food Programme (WFP). Much of the food donated is genetically modified.' Mr Walsh's article implies a conspiracy between the United States government and the WFP to dump unsafe, American GM crops into the one remaining unquestioning market – emergency aid for the world's starving and displaced. Of greater concern to Mr Walsh should be the fact that international support for emergency food aid declined from about 10 million tons in 1994 to about 7.7 million tons in 1998.

Wheat and wheat flour account for more than half of global food aid and there are no varieties of GM wheat on the market at present. WFP only accepts food donations that comply with safety standards in the donor country. In the USA the regulatory agencies judge GM foods to be safe. The fact that the European Union has placed a two-year moratorium on GM imports is not due to food safety but rather to consumer concerns, which are largely the result of unsubstantiated 'scare-mongering' by GM opponents (see Chapters 5 and 6).

In an article in *Fortune* magazine of 21 February 2000, Gordon Conway, President of the Rockefeller Foundation, commented on a meeting with President Mugabe of Zimbabwe. The President asked Conway what he though about the Prince of Wales telling him that Africa could be fed with organic food. Conway replied that organic farming requires ongoing enrichment of the soil with organic matter. Crop yields are currently far too low to provide much leftover material to replenish the soil. Livestock in Africa are generally not very fit and produce poor quality manure, much of which is burned for fuel. Conway predicted that Africa might be able to afford the luxury of organic farming within about fifteen years, but only if the soil was first enriched with large quantities of nitrogen in the form of inorganic fertilisers.

Ironically, much of the developing world does indeed practise organic farming – they simply cannot afford chemicals. However, organic farming is not sustainable in the face of current population levels. Worse still, farming pressure on marginal lands is increasing, precisely where the environment can tolerate it the least. Simple arithmetic tells us that taking more out of the system than you put in will run the system down. In order to reverse the problem of land degradation, it is important to raise crops on land, that is suited to their cultivation. Biotechnology can enhance the yield potential of productive land, so that marginal land can remain uncultivated and revert to a more pristine condition.

GM crops in South Africa

Let us now look at the status of GM crops in South Africa. Figure 25 shows the number of applications for GM permits received between 1990 and July 1999. The South African Genetic Experimentation Committee (SAGENE) handled these applications prior to the implementation of the GMO Act towards the end of 1999.

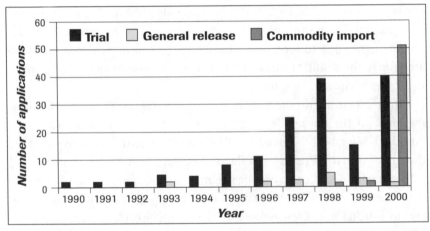

FIGURE 25: Total numbers of applications for GM permits in South Africa from 1990 to 2000.

The drop in trials and general releases in 1999 is largely attributable to the fact that SAGENE had by then ceased to function effectively. The GMO Act was supposed to supersede SAGENE but this, in fact, did not happen until 2000.

Figure 26 indicates the crops considered for GMO permits during the same period. The vast majority of permit applications were for cotton and maize, followed by soybean and various micro-organisms.

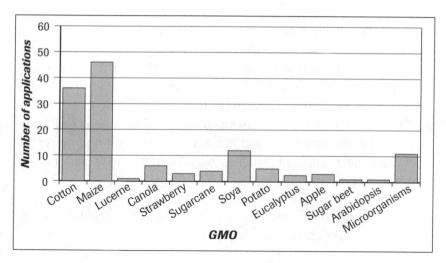

FIGURE 26: Applications for GM permits by crop in South Africa from 1990 to July 1999.

It is interesting to note the increase in the number of small-scale farmers who have been planting GM insect-resistant cotton in the Makhatini Flats area of KwaZulu-Natal during the past few years. In 1997 only four farmers took part in field trials. In 1998, 75 farmers planted 200 hectares of *Bt* cotton. In 1999 the number of farmers increased to 410 and the area to 798 hectares. In 2000, 644 farmers planted 1 250 hectares, which was approximately 50% of the total area planted to cotton in that region (J. Webster, Executive Director of AfricaBio, personal communication, 2001).

Some critics of agricultural biotechnology are concerned that it will lead to a loss of **biodiversity**. South African readers will be interested to learn that one of the world's most exciting research projects on the increase in biodiversity resulting from the use of GM insect-resistant cotton is underway on our very doorstep. It began when inspectors monitoring field trials of *Bt* cotton in KwaZulu-Natal noticed increased numbers and varieties of insects in these fields compared with the non-*Bt* cotton fields where spraying with insecticides continued as normal. They also noticed an increase in insectivorous birds and observed that birds were actually starting to nest in the *Bt* cotton fields. These observations occurred very early on in the trials and as a result we could establish a 'base-line' of insect numbers and diversity. The distribution of birds was already available in the superb *Atlas of Southern African Birds* published in 1997 by BirdLife,

South Africa and the Avian Demography Unit at the University of Cape Town. Research is currently underway to track the increase in insect and bird diversity resulting from the introduction of GM insect-resistant cotton.

Readers may also be interested in just how much plant biodiversity is retained in agricultural research institutions worldwide. For instance, the International Centre for Maize and Wheat holds 136 637 different varieties of maize and wheat and the International Institute for Tropical Agriculture holds 39 756 varieties of yam, rice, maize and cassava (Hoisington *et al.*, 1999).

Biodiversity: the variety of life on earth; includes genetic diversity within species as well as the diversity between species and ecosystems.

In summary ...

Africa needs GM crops as part of its quest for sustainable agriculture and in order to feed its population. There is no doubt that we need to improve transportation so that available food can be distributed more efficiently. We must stop wars and end corruption so that food aid ends up in the right hands. And we must curtail population growth. We need to do all this and more, but we also need GM crops.

Europe has enough food and may not want GM technology, but this does not mean that the developing world should be forced to do without it. It is important to keep an open mind on the subject, so let us not reject GM crops and foods simply because other countries do not want them.

Notes

[1] Quoted by Norman Borlaug in a speech in Lilongwe, Malawi, March 30, 2000.

[2] Quoted by Norman Borlaug in an open letter to the Editor of *The Independent*, April 10, 2000.

References and further reading

Anon. (1999) Access issues may determine whether agri-biotech will help the world's poor. *Nature*. Vol. 402, pp. 341–344.

Conway, G. (1997) *The Doubly Green Revolution: food for all in the twenty-first century*. Penguin, Ithaca, N.Y.

Dyson, T. (1999) World food trends and prospects for 2025. *Proceedings of the National Academy of Sciences*, USA. Vol. 96, pp. 5929–5936.

Harrison, J. A., Allan, D. G., Underhill, L. G., Herremans, M., Tree, A. J., Parker, V. and Brown, C. J. (eds) (1997) *The Atlas of Southern African Birds*. BirdLife South Africa and the Avian Demography Unit, Johannesburg.

Hoisington, D., Khairallah, M., Reeves, T., Ribaut, J-M., Skovmand, B., Taba, S. and Warburton, M. (1999) Plant genetic resources: what can they contribute toward increased crop productivity? *Proceedings of the National Academy of Sciences*, USA. Vol. 96, pp. 5937–5943.

Qaim, M. (1999) The economic effects of genetically modified orphan commodities: projections for sweet potato in Kenya. *ISAAA Brief*. No. 13. ISAAA, Ithaca, N.Y.

Krattiger, A. (1998) The importance of agri-biotechnology for global prosperity. *ISAAA Brief*. No. 6. ISAAA, Ithaca, N.Y.

Wambugu, F. (1999) Why Africa needs agricultural biotech. *Nature*. Vol. 400, pp. 15–16.

World Bank. (2000) *Can Africa claim the twenty-first century?* World Bank, Washington, DC.

Chapter 11

A look into the future

A global review

According to a report published in 2000, the world's four principal crops at that time were soybean, maize, cotton and canola (James, 2000a). In 2000 15% of these crops were transgenic varieties. This represents 44.2 million hectares, which is equivalent to almost twice the total land area of the United Kingdom. The increase in area of transgenic crops between 1999 and 2000 was 11%, equivalent to 4.3 million hectares. This increase is about one quarter of the corresponding increase of 12.1 million hectares between 1998 and 1999. Of this, 3.6 million hectares, equivalent to 84%, was in developing countries.

GM varieties comprise 30% of total soybeans planted globally, 8% of maize, 10% of cotton and 14% of canola. The three most widely adopted GM traits are herbicide tolerance, insect resistance and a combination of insect resistance and herbicide tolerance. Thirteen countries have contributed to this increase: eight are industrialised nations and five are from the developing world. In China alone, within a period of two years, more than 1.5 million small-scale farmers were growing on average 0.15 hectares of insect-resistant *Bt* cotton. Argentina tops the list of developing countries planting GM crops, with a total of 10 million hectares in 2000. This represented an increase of 49% over the plantings in 1999. Of the four countries that grew 99% of the global transgenic crop area, the USA grew 68%, Argentina 23%, Canada 7% and China 1%. Nine countries together grew the other 1%, with South Africa and Australia being the only countries in that group growing more than 100 000 hectares of transgenic crops.

Globally, transgenic crops have been adopted at a dramatic rate since 1995. Figure 27 shows this graphically, with the area planted to GM crops increasing by 44% between 1998 and 1999.

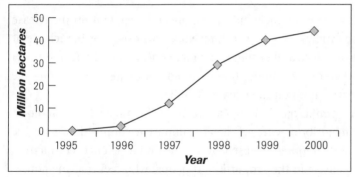

FIGURE 27: Global area of transgenic crops.
(Source: James, 2000b)

The value of the global market for GM seed grew from $1 million in 1995 to an estimated $2.7–3 billion in 1999. We expected these increases to plateau in 2000, partly due to the lack of public acceptance particularly in Europe. However, James (2000b) showed an increase in global plantings of GM crops of more than 10% in 2000 compared with 1999. The USDA in the USA recently projected similar increases for the 2001 season (http://usda.mannlib.cornell.edu/reports/nassr/field/pcp-bbp/). In future we expect a shift towards the development of second generation GM crops with 'output' quality traits described in Chapter 4. Whether this will lead to greater consumer acceptance of foods derived from GM crops remains to be seen.

Data from a survey carried out in November 1999 and published by the International Research Group on Biotechnology and the Public (2000) suggested that Europeans have become increasingly opposed to GM foods. However, they remain supportive of medical and environmental applications of biotechnology. In general, where the public perceives genuine moral difficulties and no real benefits, it is unwilling to accept the perceived risks of new biotechnologies.

However, a change appears to have occurred. A document published by the European Parliament (2001) shows resolve to support the development of biotechnology in the European Union. The European Parliament also expects the biotechnology industry to be placed prominently on the agenda of the next European Council. The report further states that it regrets government actions that have blocked or delayed authorisation of GM products for reasons not based on objective scientific opinion. It observes that the existing *de facto* moratorium does particular harm to small and medium-sized enterprises in the European Union. It welcomes the agreement reached

CHAPTER 11: A LOOK INTO THE FUTURE

between the European Council and the European Parliament on the release of GMOs and considers that a clear framework now exists for the release of GMOs in Europe, which will ensure maximum consumer and environmental protection. It therefore concludes that it would not be justified to continue the *de facto* moratorium on the release of GMOs.

In the USA public opinion appears to be divided over biotechnology. Although the majority of citizens remain supportive, opposition is on the rise (Priest, 2000). Figures released by the National Science Foundation show a small increase in the proportion of people who feel that the potential adverse effects of genetic engineering outweigh the clear benefits. Resistance increased from 20% in 1995 to 29% in 1999.

A survey carried out in Japan shows that support for biotechnology is declining, although it remains higher than in the USA or Europe (Macer and Ng, 2000). Parallel surveys of scientists showed that 72% believed that genetic engineering would improve the quality of life.

Opportunities for the future

A particularly interesting application of transgenic plants, which may positively influence attitudes towards GM crops, is their use in **bioremediation** to remove metals from contaminated soils (see Chapter 5). **Phytoremediation,** or bioremediation using plants, is a potentially cheap way of removing contaminating metals such as mercury, lead and chromium.

In future we will see continued work on the use of transgenic plants as factories for vaccine production. Part of these efforts will be to produce edible vaccines, probably in the form of dried products such as bananas and tomatoes. Plants also offer unique alternatives for the bulk production of vaccines. Producing vaccines in plants rather than in animal cells removes the potential for contamination by animal viruses that could cause diseases in humans. Using plants is also considerably cheaper. Tobacco, in particular, is a remarkably robust crop that we could use for this purpose. Anyone who has visited a tobacco-producing country during a drought period will have noticed that even if no other crop can grow, tobacco will!

> **Bioremediation:** the use of biological organisms to improve the quality of soil, water or air.

174

Phytoremediation: the use of plants to improve the quality of soil, water or air.

And what is the future of hemp? *Cannabis sativa* is the source of marijuana, but its fibre makes excellent rope and linen-like fabrics. It has huge agricultural potential for producing useful proteins due to the fact that it has almost no known diseases or pests. It also grows in the most inhospitable soils and climates. The idea is vastly appealing that we may one day convert these two plant species, tobacco and hemp, which currently produce habit-forming drugs, into plants that produce health-promoting pharmaceuticals.

So what are the chances for GM crops and foods in the future? If this new technology is to deliver the benefits outlined in this book, it will need broad public acceptance and support. Governments, industry, scientists and everyone involved in its development will have to learn to become effective communicators. It is only through knowledge and understanding that the public will gain confidence in GM crops and foods. We need an informed society that understands the impact of this technology on the environment, on food safety, on sustainable agriculture and on global food security. This book is one scientist's effort to facilitate this process.

References and further reading

European Parliament. (2001) *European Parliament report on the future of the biotechnology industry.* (2000/2100[INI]) RR\297119EN.doc. 28 February 2001.

International Research Group on Biotechnology and the Public. (2000) Biotechnology and the European public. *Nature Biotechnology.* Vol. 18, pp. 935–938.

James, C. (2000a) Global status of commercialized transgenic crops: 1999. *ISAAA Brief.* No. 17. ISAAA, Ithaca, N.Y.

James, C. (2000b) Global review of commercialized transgenic crops: 2000. *ISAAA Brief.* No. 21. ISAAA, Ithaca, N.Y.

Macer, D. and Ng, M. A. C. (2000) Changing attitudes to biotechnology in Japan. *Nature Biotechnology.* Vol. 18, pp. 945–947.

Priest, S. H. (2000) US public opinion divided over biotechnology? *Nature Biotechnology.* Vol. 18, pp. 939–942.

Appendix I

Testing GM foods for allergens

In May/June 2000 the World Health Organisation and the Food and Agricultural Organisation convened an expert consultation on food derived from biotechnology (http://www.who.int). S. Taylor suggested an alternative approach to the testing of allergens in foods outlined in Chapter 5, Figure 17. His proposal (see Figure 28) is adapted from the 'decision tree' method proposed by Metcalfe et al. (1996) whereby decisions can be taken

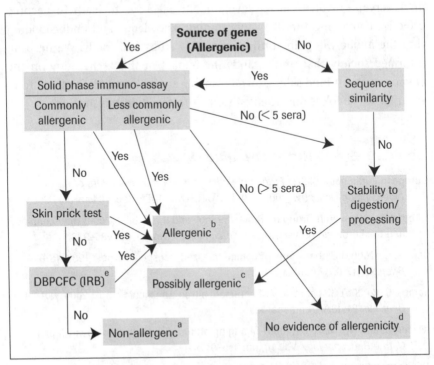

FIGURE 28: Assessment of the allergenic potential of foods derived from GM crop plants. (*Source: Adapted from Metcalfe* et al. *1996*)

in a step-by-step manner. The decision tree strategy focuses on:

- the source of the gene;
- similarities between the amino acid sequences of the newly introduced protein and known allergens;
- physicochemical properties of the newly introduced protein, including the effect of pH and/or digestion (most allergens are resistant to gastric acidity and to digestive enzymes that degrade proteins);
- immunochemical reactivity of the newly introduced protein with IgE, the antibody associated with allergic reactions (the antibody is extracted from the blood serum of individuals known to be allergic to the source of the transferred genetic material); and
- heat or processing stability (allergens denatured during cooking or other food processing are of less concern).

Reference

Metcalfe, D. D., Astwood, J. D., Townsend, R., Sampson, H. A., Taylor, S. L. and Fuchs, R. L. (1996) Assessment of the allergenic potential of foods derived from genetically engineered crop plants. *Critical Reviews in Food, Science and Nutrition.* Vol. 36, pp. S165–S186.

Notes to Figure 29

a   The combination of tests involving allergic human subjects or blood serum from such subjects provides a high level of confidence that no major allergens have been transferred. The only remaining uncertainty is the likelihood of a minor allergen affecting a small percentage of the population allergic to the source material.

b   Any positive results from tests involving allergic human subjects or blood serum from such subjects suggest that the novel protein is a potential allergen. Foods containing such novel proteins should be labelled to protect allergic consumers.

c   A novel protein with no amino acid sequence similarity to known allergens, but stable to digestion and processing, should be considered a possible allergen. Further evaluation is necessary to address this uncertainty. The nature of the tests is determined on a case-by-case basis.

d   A novel protein with no sequence similarity to known allergens and not stable to digestion and processing shows no evidence of allergenicity. However, the level of confidence based on only two decision criteria is modest. Other criteria, such as the level of expression of the introduced protein, should also be considered.

e   DBPCFC = double-blind placebo-controlled food challenge; IRB = institutional review board: an ethical review process, involving community members, which ensures proper patient information and guards against coercion.

APPENDIX I: TESTING FOODS FOR ALLERGENS

Appendix II

Horizontal gene transfer

Gene transfer from a GM plant to a bacterium or to humans or animals is called horizontal gene transfer. It is the movement of genetic information between sexually unrelated organisms (different species). This is in contrast to vertical gene transfer that occurs from parent to offspring.

In this section we consider the evidence for horizontal gene transfer and the possible consequences should it occur:

1. The process of gene transfer from transgenic food to intestinal bacteria and the consequences thereof, using the feeding of transgenic maize to ruminants (cows and sheep) as an example.
2. Concern around the presence of antibiotic resistance genes in transgenic maize, using the *bla* gene (encoding resistance to certain antibiotics such as ampicillin) as an example; this gene was used as a selectable marker in the generation of one of the early GM maize varieties.
3. Other antibiotic resistance genes and their transfer to micro-organisms in the environment.
4. Evidence for DNA uptake in the human oral cavity and the potential for transfer of bacterial DNA to mammalian cells.

> *bla* **gene:** a gene that codes for resistance to certain antibiotics, such as ampicillin.

1. Gene transfer from transgenic food to intestinal bacteria

Excise transgenic DNA from the maize chromosome

When scientists produce a GM crop, they insert the required gene (segment of DNA) into a plant chromosome. In order for this length of introduced DNA to be transferred from the plant to another organism, it must be excised from the chromosome. We can do this by 'looping out' the DNA to reconstitute a plasmid. This is a small autonomous circle of DNA that carries the foreign gene. The gene can also be excised from the plant cell as a linear fragment of DNA. See Figure 29 on the next page for an illustration of the following three processes of horizontal gene transfer:

- *Homologous recombination* can result in the looping out of DNA. This is recombination between the same or very similar regions of DNA and it occurs between adjacent copies of tandemly integrated DNA. Tandem integration events take place during the biolistic procedure used to introduce foreign genes into monocot plants such as maize.
- The inserted DNA can also be excised by *illegitimate recombination*, which does not require homologous DNA sequences.
- A more likely event is the generation of *linear fragments* by enzymatic cleavage or by chemical or physical breakage of plant DNA. This results in a random assortment of fragments that represent the whole genome.

In organisms we have studied, such as tobacco, the frequency of *homologous recombination* ranges from less than one event a million cells to about one event in 10 000 cells (Peterhans *et al.*, 1990). In other words, no more than one in 10 000 maize cells will contain a complete plasmid, although each maize plant consists of millions of cells.

Excision by *illegitimate recombination* should be even less frequent. The formation of DNA circles has been demonstrated in a yeast, but a careful literature search (Schulter *et al.*, 1995) failed to identify any studies demonstrating a similar phenomenon in maize DNA. A study attempting to detect transfer of a plasmid from a transgenic potato to the plant pathogenic bacterium, *Erwinia chrysanthemi*, also failed (*ibid.*).

The fate of DNA released from maize kernels during digestion

DNA released from maize kernels, either in the living plant or during preparation of feed, comes into contact with enzymes called plant nucleases that break it down. Once ingested, similar enzymes from various animal tissues including the salivary glands, pancreas and intestine also attack the DNA. These enzymes cleave most of the DNA into small *linear fragments*.

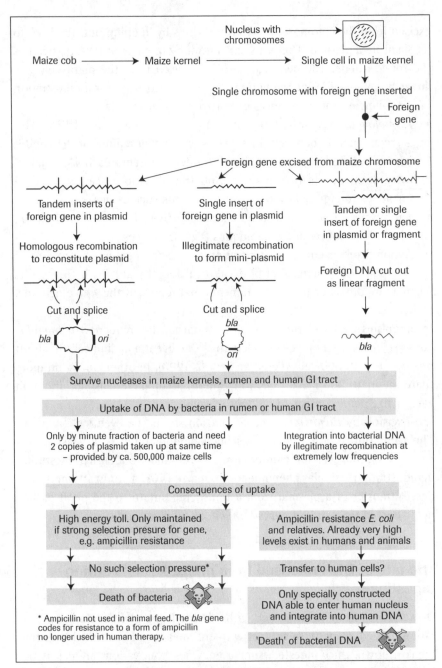

FIGURE 29: The steps that would have to be taken for DNA to be transferred horizontally from GM plants to bacteria and to animals or humans.

The smallest fragment of DNA that could contain the *bla* gene is about 900 base pairs (bp) in length. In addition, the fragment of DNA containing the plasmid's replication region (origin of replication or *ori* in Figure 29) carries about 1 600 pairs of bases. Nucleases in maize cells are so active that they can degrade DNA to fragments of less than 500 bp within an hour. In the laboratory, scientists use strong protein denaturing agents to eliminate nuclease activity so that they can obtain large pieces of DNA from plant cells (Ausubel *et al.*, 1992). These agents are not present in the rumen.

Uptake of released DNA by bacteria in the rumen

Some bacteria can take up DNA from the environment by natural transformation. The double-stranded DNA binds to the bacterial cell surface, is nicked, and one strand is degraded. Accordingly, a single strand of DNA enters the bacterium. So far, despite numerous attempts, there have been no reports of naturally transformable bacteria in the predominant species of rumen bacteria. Most of these bacteria are obligate anaerobes that can only survive in the absence of oxygen (Salyers, 1998).

In the unlikely event that a plasmid were released from a maize cell as described above, it would only replicate in certain bacteria, such as *E. coli* and some of its close relatives. In natural transformation, bacterial cells take up single-stranded DNA. At least two copies of a plasmid must therefore be introduced simultaneously into the same bacterial cell in order to provide overlapping segments to regenerate the plasmid (*ibid.*).

Slim chances

Imagine that one in 10 000 maize cells contained excised plasmid DNA. If, say, 4% of the released DNA survived nuclease attack, over 500 000 (25 x 20 000) maize cells would have to be present in the rumen at the same time to provide these two plasmids.

Bacteria carrying such plasmids experience a high energy toll and only strong selection can keep these rumen bacteria growing in such a competitive environment. Although antibiotics such as ampicillin are used to treat some infections in farm animals, they are no longer one of the major antibiotics added to feed in Europe. The selection pressure for bacteria containing the ampicillin resistance gene is therefore limited.

APPENDIX II: HORIZONTAL GENE TRANSFER

Bear in mind that DNA uptake is a random event. The *bla* gene therefore competes for transfer into a bacterium with the rest of the DNA in the plant genome as well as DNA from other dietary sources. The maize genome is about one million times larger than most plasmids, so only a millionth of the DNA released from transgenic maize will be plasmid DNA.

It appears most likely that bacterial cells will take up DNA released from transgenic maize in the form of linear fragments. These will be incorporated into the bacterial genome by illegitimate recombination, which occurs at even lower frequencies than homologous recombination. Illegitimate recombination is as likely to integrate a fragment of a gene as an intact gene (see Figure 29 on page 180).

Expression of the *bla* gene

If rumen bacteria are transformed, will the *bla* gene be expressed? This will occur only in *E. coli* and close relatives, but not in any anaerobic rumen bacteria tested so far (Salyers, 1998). Any other bacterium will have to acquire new genetic elements in order to express the *bla* gene. These elements are promoters that inform an organism that the 'gene starts here'. The cell can obtain them by mutation or by the transposition of a promoter from another gene. These would, however, be extremely rare events.

2. Antibiotic resistance genes in transgenic maize

Gene transfer from GM feed to rumen bacteria?

We can do experiments to determine the potential for genetic transfer from transgenic feed to rumen bacteria. Scientists at the University of Leeds are doing just that and have presented their preliminary results (Coughlan, 2000). They fed chickens GM maize for five days but to date have been unable to isolate gut bacteria that have incorporated and expressed the *bla* gene. They also added DNA to silage effluent, saliva and rumen fluid taken from sheep but found no uptake by bacteria in the normal flora of the rumen, saliva or silage. However, the experiments are not over and have yet to be published.

Although the risk of rumen bacteria acquiring and expressing the *bla* gene from transgenic maize is extremely low, it is not impossible. We must therefore consider the consequences of such acquisition. In particular, how will such bacteria add to the already high incidence of ampicillin-resistant bacteria in natural isolates?

Naturally occurring ampicillin resistance

Over 70% of *E. coli* isolated from diseased calves and nearly 20% from diseased adult cattle are ampicillin-resistant. More than 60% of *Salmonella typhimurium* bacteria from adult cattle are similarly resistant (Salyers, 1998). However, this is not universally the case and there are wide-ranging reports of resistance, down to as little as 1% (Courvalin, 1998). In groundwater in rural Tennessee 69% of isolates, mostly enterics, were ampicillin-resistant (McKeon *et al.*, 1995). Almost all children studied in Mexico carry resistant *E. coli* strains (Calva *et al.*, 1996). Thus although levels of resistance do vary, ampicillin resistance is widespread in *E. coli* and enteric bacteria. Thus, it seems more rational to be concerned about the overuse of antibiotics, both on the farm and in human medicine, than to worry about the unproven and probably infinitesimally small risk that new copies of the *bla* gene could enter bacteria from transgenic maize feed.

Note also that the *bla* gene used in the development of some types of transgenic maize codes for one of the early forms of β-lactamase. Since then extensive research and development has produced more potent forms (Medeiros, 1997). It is true that many of these new genes are derived from mutations of the original *bla* gene. Similar mutations could occur in a ruminant organism that has acquired the *bla* gene. However, such evolution would take a decade or two with intensive selection (Salyers, 1998).

3. Transfer of other antibiotic resistance genes to micro-organisms

Rumen bacteria and antibiotic resistance

Let us now consider concerns that rumen bacteria might acquire genes other than ampicillin resistance. One example is the *nptII* gene encoding

APPENDIX II: HORIZONTAL GENE TRANSFER

resistance to kanamycin and neomycin. This gene has been included in certain transgenic procedures to select transformed plant cells. Accordingly it is designed to be expressed in plants and would have to acquire genetic elements to allow it to be expressed in bacteria.

Neither kanamycin nor neomycin is unique for any disease. They are infrequently used antibiotics that are rarely administered orally. They are also not used in agriculture to any great extent. Thus there is minimal selection pressure for the development of resistant bacteria. A World Health Organisation workshop in 1993 concluded that the use of the *nptII* genes in GM plants presents no health risks to people (WHO, 1993).

Soil bacteria and antibiotic resistance

What about the transfer of antibiotic resistance genes to micro-organisms in the soil? Sikorski *et al.* (1998) have transformed bacteria by loading non-sterile soil with the soil bacterium, *Pseudomonas stutzeri*, together with its own DNA. Success was extremely time-dependent, presumably due to the presence of soil nucleases. However, addition of cells three days after DNA loading still yielded 3% of the initial numbers of transformed cells.

No one has been able to show that soil bacteria take up expressible antibiotic resistance genes when exposed to transgenic plant material under natural conditions. However, Gebhard and Smalla (1998) were able to detect horizontal gene transfer under laboratory conditions using the soil bacterium *Acinetobacter*, a species with an inherently high transformation frequency. Whether this could occur in nature needs to be tested. So far, all studies on gene transfer from plants to soil micro-organisms *in situ* have shown that, if such events occur at all, they do so at extremely low frequencies (Dröge *et al.*, 1998).

Finally, there is no selective advantage for genes such as *bla* and *nptII* in transformed soil bacteria. Therefore it is unlikely that the traits would be maintained. Furthermore, resistance to antibiotics and herbicides is already widespread among soil microbes, because of selection pressure from naturally occurring antibiotic-producing fungi and bacteria, and because of repeated applications of herbicides.

Alternatives to antibiotic marker genes

Although the *bla* and *nptII* genes are considered safe, there is pressure on scientists to come up with alternative marker genes that can select for transformed plant material but not encode resistance to antibiotics. One such gene codes for an enzyme (phospho-mannose isomerase or PMI) that breaks down a sugar-phosphate compound (mannose-6-phosphate). This compound inhibits the growth of many plants excluding legumes such as peas and beans. Plant cells lacking this enzyme are unable to survive in tissue culture medium containing the sugar-phosphate. A group of Danish scientists has cloned and developed the gene coding for PMI (Joersbo, 1998).

4. Uptake of DNA in the human oral cavity and intestine

Can DNA from transgenic foods be absorbed in the oral cavity? This is one of the most complex and heterogeneous microbial habitats in the human body and certain oral bacteria are naturally competent for transformation. Recently, Mercer *et al.* (1999) have shown that very high concentrations of DNA exposed to degradation by human saliva in a test tube, were able to transform the naturally competent oral bacterium *Streptococcus gordonii*. These results, however, need to be reproduced *in vivo*, as DNA decay in ˙ saliva is rapid and the transformation frequency is expected to change in proportion to the square of the DNA concentration. Naked DNA is predicted to have little chance of survival under conditions prevailing lower down the digestive tract (as was discussed above for ruminants).

In vivo: in a living organism (Latin vivum = life).

Transfer of bacterial DNA to mammalian cells

All foods contain DNA and, although we have not accurately determined the amount that consumers ingest on a daily basis, estimates for cows indicate that they consume approximately 600 milligrams of DNA per day

(Beever and Kemp, 2000). Any concerns regarding the presence of novel DNA in GM-derived foods must take into consideration that the DNA from this source would represent less than 1/250 000 of the total amount of DNA consumed. In view of this and the digestibility of dietary DNA, there is an extremely low probability of transfer of genes from GM plants to mammalian cells. It is nonetheless necessary to examine the possibility.

Numerous experiments have evaluated the possibility of transfer of bacterial DNA to mammalian cells, but to date there have been no reports of such transfer. Schubbert *et al.* (1998) reported that oral administration of high doses of bacterially-derived DNA to pregnant mice resulted in fragments of this DNA being detected in relatively few cells of 15% of fetal and newborn progeny. This DNA was, however, not expressed. Transfer occurred via the placenta and not through the germline cells. Beever and Kemp (2000) have seriously questioned the significance of these observations and concluded that they do not demonstrate that bacterial DNA can be transferred to, or stably maintained in, mammalian cells.

Despite repeated efforts, attempts to demonstrate plasmid transfer from bacteria to mammalian cells have been unsuccessful (Grillot-Courvalin *et al.*, 1998). These authors showed that *E. coli* bacteria are able to transfer specifically designed plasmid DNA into mammalian nuclei, as long as they manage to invade mammalian cells and lyse, releasing their DNA. By contrast, and extremely significantly, they could not detect *E. coli* chromosomal DNA in such cells. Thus only DNA designed to enter mammalian nuclei is able to do so; the rest of the foreign DNA cannot.

Conclusions

The above evidence supports the conclusion that, while horizontal gene transfer can and has occurred, such events are rare and need to be seen in the context of evolutionary time. Even very rare events may have an ecological impact if the transferred gene increases the fitness of the recipient bacterium or cell. Hence, the genes encoded by the transferred DNA in the GM plant should be the focus of bio-safety considerations rather than the transfer process itself.

In the cases of *bla* and *nptII* referred to in this appendix, the chances of increasing the ecological fitness of bacteria acquiring the genes from

186 –

transgenic plant material are remote. The incidence of natural populations of bacteria having similar antibiotic resistance genes is already very high. The risk that any bacteria could receive these genes from a plant and express them is extremely low. There is no evidence that such an event has occurred, even under ideal laboratory conditions. Finally, there is no known risk associated with the remote possibility that these genes could transform mammalian cells and express proteins.

When scientists assess the safety of expressed proteins for the purpose of registering GM crops, they consider all genes on a case-by-case basis. The introduced genes represent a few of the 20 000 to 40 000 genes found in the crop plants. The probability of transferring any of the GM genes is no greater than that of transferring any of the other genes in the plants. However, a key consideration in the registration process is a thorough assessment of the safety of the proteins for which the genes code. If the protein products are safe, in the extremely unlikely event of horizontal gene transfer, they should not pose a risk to consumers or to the environment if produced by transformed microbes.

Although the use of antibiotic resistance genes in currently available transgenic crops is considered safe, there is public perception that they could add to the already high levels of antibiotic resistance in pathogenic bacteria. Despite the fact that there is no scientific evidence to support this, scientists and regulators working in this field agree that they should use alternative transformation technologies that do not introduce antibiotic resistance genes into GM crops and foods. Considerable progress is being made in achieving this aim.

References and further reading

Ausubel, F. M., Brent, R., Kingston, R. E., Moore, D. D., Seidman, J. G., Smith, J. and Struhl, K. (1992) *Current protocols in Molecular Biology.* Greene Publishing Associates and John Wiley and Sons, New York.

Beever D. E. and Kemp, C. F. (2000) Safety issues associated with the DNA in animal feed derived from genetically modified crops. A review of scientific and regulatory procedures. *Nutrition Abstracts and Reviews.* Vol. 70, pp. 175–182.

Calva, J. J., Sifuentes-Osornio, J. and Ceron, C. (1996) Anti-microbial resistance in fecal flora: longitudinal community-based surveillance of children from urban Mexico. *Antimicrobial Agents and Chemotherapy.* Vol. 40, pp. 1699–1702.

Coughlan, A. (2000) So far so good: for the moment, the gene genie is staying in its bottle. *New Scientist.* Vol. 2231, p. 4.

Courvalin, P. (1998) Plantes transgeniques et antibiotiques. *La Recherche*. Vol. 309, pp. 36–40.

Dröge, M., Pühler, A. and Selbitschka, W. (1998) Horizontal gene transfer as a biosafety issue: a natural phenomenon of public concern. *Journal of Biotechnology*. Vol. 64, pp. 75–90.

Gebhard, F. and Smalla, K. (1998) Transformation of *Acinetobacter* sp. strain BD413 by transgenic sugar beet DNA. *Applied and Environmental Microbiology*. Vol. 64, pp. 1550–1554.

Grillot-Courvalin, C., Goussard, S., Huetz, F., Ojcius, D. M. and Courvalin, P. (1998) Functional gene transfer from intracellular bacteria to mammalian cells. *Nature Biotechnology*. Vol. 16, pp. 862–866.

Joersbo, M. (1998) Analysis of mannose selection used for transformation of sugar beet. *Molecular Breeding*. Vol. 4, pp. 111–117.

McKeon, D. M., Calabrese, J. P. and Bissonnette, G. K. (1995) Antibiotic resistant Gram-negative bacteria in rural groundwater supplies. *Water Research*. Vol. 29, pp. 1902–1908.

Medeiros, A. A. (1997) Evolution and dissemination of ß-lactamases accelerated by generations of ß-lactam antibiotics. *Clinical and Infectious Diseases*. Vol. 24, pp. S19–S45.

Mercer, D. K., Scott, K. P., Bruce-Johnson, W. A., Glover L. A. and Flint, H. J. (1999) Fate of free DNA and transformation of the oral bacterium *Streptococcus gordonii* DL1 by plasmid DNA in human saliva. *Applied and Environmental Microbiology*. Vol. 65, pp. 6–10.

Peterhans A., Schlupmann, H., Basse, C. and Paszkowski, J. (1990) Intrachromosomal recombination in plants. *European Molecular Biology Organisation (EMBO) Journal*. Vol. 9, pp. 3437–3445.

Salyers, A. (1998) Genetically engineered foods: safety issues associated with antibiotic resistance genes. (http//www.healthsci.tufts.edu/apua/salyersreport.htm)

Schubbert R., Hohlweg, U., Renz, D. and Doerfler, W. (1998) On the fate of orally ingested foreign DNA in mice: chromosomal association and placental transmission of the fetus. *Molecular and General Genetics*. Vol. 259, pp. 569–576.

Schulter, K., Futterer, F. and Potrykus, I. (1995) 'Horizontal' gene transfer from a transgenic potato line to a bacterial pathogen (*Erwinia chrysanthemi*) occurs – if at all – at an extremely low frequency. *Nature Biotechnology*. Vol. 13, pp.1094–1098.

Sikorski, J., Graupner, S., Lorenz, M. G. and Wackernagel, W. (1998) Natural genetic transformation of *Pseudomonas stutzeri* in a non-sterile soil. *Microbiology*. Vol. 144, pp. 569–576.

Thomson, J. A. (2001) Horizontal transfer of DNA from GM crops to bacteria and to mammalian cells. *Journal of Food Science*. Vol. 66, pp. 188-193.

WHO (1993) Health aspects of markers in GM plants. Report of a WHO workshop. WHO/FNU/FOS/93.6. World Health Organisation, Geneva.

Appendix III

International food safety assessment documents

FAO/WHO. (1996) Biotechnology and food safety. Report of a Joint JAO/WHO Consultation. FAO, Food and Nutrition Paper 61.

FAO/WHO. (2000) Safety aspects of genetically modified foods of plant origin. Report of a Joint FAO/WHO Expert Consultation on foods derived from biotechnology, 29 May – 2 June 2000.

IFBC (International Food Biotechnology Council). (1991). Biotechnologies and food: assuring the safety of foods produced by genetic modification. *Regulatory Toxicology and Pharmacology*. Vol. 12, pp. SI–SI96.

Kuiper, H. A., Kleter, G. A., Noteborn, H. P. J. M. and Kok, E. J. (2001) Assessment of the food safety issues related to genetically modified foods. *The Plant Journal*. Vol. 27, pp. 503–528.

Metcalfe, D. D., Astwood, J. D., Townsend, R., Sampson, H. A., Taylor, S. L. and Fuchs, R. L. (1996) Assessment of the allergenic potential of foods derived from genetically engineered crop plants. *Critical Reviews in Food Science and Nutrition*. Vol. 36(S), pp. S165–186.

OECD (Organisation for Economic Cooperation and Development). (1993) *Safety evaluation of foods produced by modern biotechnology: concepts and principles*. OECD, Paris.

OECD. (1996) OECD Documents: Food safety evaluation. OECD, Paris.

OECD. (1997) OECD Documents. *Report of the OECD Workshop on the toxicological and nutritional testing of novel foods*. OECD, Paris.

WHO (World Health Organisation). (1991) Strategies for assessing the safety of foods produced by biotechnology. Report of a Joint FAO/WHO Consultation. World Health Organisation, Geneva.

WHO. (1993) Health aspects of marker genes in genetically modified plants. Report of a WHO Workshop. World Health Organisation, Geneva. WHO/FNU/FOS/93.6.

WHO. (1995) Application of the principles of substantial equivalence to the safety evaluation of foods and food components from plants derived by modern biotechnology. Report of a WHO Workshop. World Health Organisation, Geneva. WHO/FNU/FOS/95.1

Appendix IV

Web pages of interest

Advisory Committee on Releases to the Environment (UK Department of the Environment, Transport and the Regions), **http://www.environment.detr.gov.uk/acre**

AfricaBio: a South African organisation that disseminates information on biotechnology, **http://www.africabio.com**

AgBioForum: A magazine devoted to the economics and management of agro-biotechnology, **http://www.agbioforum.org**

AgBiotechNet: hot topics put together on biotech and developing countries, giving both sides of the argument, **http://www.agbiotechnet.com**

Agricultural Biotechnology: benefits of transgenic soybean, **http://ncfap.org/soy85.pdf**

Agricultural Biotechnology for Sustainable Productivity Support Project (USA): helps developing countries use and manage biotechnology, **http://www.iia.msu.edu/absp**

Agricultural Biotechnology: intellectual property and regulations, **http://www.agwest.sk.ca**

Alliance for Better Foods, **http://www.betterfoods.org**

American Crop Protection Association: studies and promotes the technical fit and environmental soundness of plant biotechnology as part of integrated crop production, **http://www.acpa.org/public/issues/biotech/about_plant_biotech.html**

BBC Channel 4 documentary on the rise and fall of GM foods: transcript, **http://www.agbioworld.org/articles/channel4.html**

Belgian Biosafety Server: regulatory information for Belgium and other European countries, **http://biosafety.ihe.be**

BioGuide: an interactive guide to biotechnology regulations in the UK, **http://dtiinfo1.dti.gov.uk/bioguide/bioguide.htm#contents**

Bioline Online Journal Biosafety: original papers on the effects of GMOs on people and the environment, **http://www.bdt.org.br/bioline/by**

BioTech Life Science Dictionary: a very useful biotechnology dictionary, **http://biotech.icmb.utexas.edu/pages/dictionary.html**

Biotechnology Industry News: a Yahoo-sponsored daily news report, **http://biz.yahoo.com/news/biotechnology.html**

Biotechnology Industry Organization: represents the biotechnology industry in the USA, **http://www.bio.org**

British Medical Association, **http://www.bma.org.uk**

Campaign to Label GM Foods, **http://www.craigwinters.com**

Centre for Global Food Issues: debunks myths, **http://www.cgfi.com**

Centre for International Development at Harvard University: provides a forum for public debate on the role of biotechnology in global society, especially as it relates to development of third world societies, **http://www.cid.harvard.edu/cidbiotech/bioconfpp/**

Consultative Group on International Agricultural Research (CGIAR): agricultural biotechnology in the developing world, **http://www.cgiar.org**

Convention on Biological Diversity: addresses all aspects of biological diversity and genetic resources, **http://www.biodiv.org**

Council for Agricultural Science and Technology (USA): position statement on food and agricultural biotechnology, **http://www.cast-science.org/biotechnology/20001011.htm**

Council for Biotechnology Information: publication of safety data for specific biotechnology products, **http://www.whybiotech.com**

CropGen: UK based pro-GMO lobby, **http://www.cropgen.org/**

CSA: hot topics on genetically modified foods, **http://www.csa.com/hottopics/gmfood/overview.html**

EFB Agri-Biotechnology (European Federation of Biotechnology): stimulates interactions between research groups and the agri-industry, helps disseminate scientific information and develop teaching aids, **http://www.agbiotech.org**

EFB Task Group on Public Perceptions of Biotechnology, **http://www.kluyver.stm.tudelft.nl/efb/tgppb/main.htm**

European Food Information Council: provides science-based information on food, **http://www.eufic.org/open/fopen.htm**

European Molecular Biology Organisation: homepage, **http://www.embo.org**

Food and Agriculture Organisation: homepage, **http://www.fao.org**

Foodbiotech: information on food biotechnology with links to specific organisations, **http://www.foodbiotech.org**

Genetically Engineered Crops for Pest Management in US Agriculture: Farm-level effects, **http://www.ers.usda.gov/epubs/pdf/aer786/aer786.pdf**

Glossary of Biotechnology Terms: online version of Technomic Publishing's Glossary, **http://biotechterms.org/**

Greenpeace on GMOs, **http://www.greenpeace.org/~geneng**

Information Systems in Biotechnology News Report: produced every month, **http://www.isb.vt.edu**

International Centre for Genetic Engineering and Biotechnology, Biosafety web pages: Safe use of biotechnology in the developing world, **http://www.icgeb.trieste.it/biosafety**

International Consumers for Civil Society (ICCS): reviews regulation of agricultural biotechnology in the United States, **http://www.icfcs.org/biotechreg.htm**

International Food Information Council: provides information on food safety and nutrition, **http://www.inicinfo.health.org/**

International Service for the Acquisition of Agri-Biotech Applications: based at Cornell University, produces regular news briefs, **http://www.isaaa.org**

Information Resource for the Release of Organisms to the Environment: provides information relevant to the release of animals, plants and micro-organisms into the environment, **http://www.bdt.org.br/bdt/irro**

Life Sciences Knowledge Center, **http://www.biotechknowledge.com**

Monarch butterfly: Mark Sears paper, **http://www.biotech-info.net/Searsreport.pdf**

Monsanto rice research web site: access to their Rice Genome Sequence Database, **http://www.rice-research.org, http://www.monsanto.com/monsanto/mediacenter/2000/00apr4_rice.html**

National Academy of Sciences of USA, **http://www.nas.edu**

National Food Processors Association, **http://www.nfpa-food.org/science/biotech.html**

New York Times: web site on GMOs, **http://www.nytimes.com/library/national/science/health/gm-index.html**

News of Agricultural Biotechnology, Environmental Safety, Food Labelling and Consumer Choice, **http://www/agcare.org/inthenews.html**

Nuffield Foundation, **http://www.nuffield.org**

Organisation for Economic Co-operation and Development (OECD): report on biotechnology, **http://www.oecd.org/subject/biotech**

Patrick Moore homepage: PhD in Ecology, was a founding member of Greenpeace but now criticises their stand on GM crops as being unscientific and extremist, **http://www.greenspirit.com**

Pesticide Action Network, **http://www.poptel.org.uk/panap**

PNAS Online, National Academy of Sciences, **http://www.pnas.org**

Rockefeller Foundation on Plant Biotechnology: Costs and benefits by Gordon Conway (President), **http://www.biotech-info.net/gordon_conway.html**

Royal Society (United Kingdom), Genetically Modified Plants for Food Use: reviews current regulatory controls in the UK and Europe and addresses environmental and human health issues, **http://www.royalsoc.ac.uk/st_pol40.htm**

Rural Advancement Foundation International: Canadian group concerned about the impact of genetically modified foods on biodiversity, **http://www.rafi.ca**

Safety of Genetically Engineered Foods, **http://www.psrast.org/defknfood.html**

Transgenic Crops – An Introduction and Resource Guide: a balanced information site, maintained by Colorado State University, with links to other sites, **http://www.colostate.edu/programs/lifesciences/TransgenicCrops**

Union of Concerned Scientists, Agricultural Biotechnology: monitors and evaluates the agricultural biotechnology and sustainable agriculture policies and regulations of the USDA, the FDA and the EPA (USA), **http://www.ucsusa.org/agriculture/index.html**

United States Congressional Committee on Science: a comprehensive report on the benefits and risks of plant biotechnology, **http://www.house.gov/science**

United States Department of Agriculture Animal and Plant Health Inspection Service (APHIS), **http://www.aphis.usda.gov/biotechnology/**

University of California, San Diego's brochure: Foods from genetically modified crops, **http://www.sdcma.org/GMFoodsBrochure.pdf**

University of Cape Town, Department of Molecular and Cell Biology, **http://www.uct.ac.za/microbiology/mcbdept.htm**

USA Food and Drug Administration: homepage, **http://www.fda.gov**

USA Environmental Protection Agency: homepage, **http://www.epa.gov**

USA Department of Agriculture: homepage, **http://www.usda.gov**

World Health Organisation: homepage, **http://www.who.int**

Index